FOREWORD (by Harry D Watson)

When I was asked to write this foreword, my immediate impulse was to contact all the people I have corresponded with over the years about the parish of Kilrenny and the Cellardyke fisherfolk, and to tell them the good news that George Gourlay's Fisher Life was to be reprinted. When I had assembled all their names and addresses, I found that they spanned four continents. It is truly remarkable how far the Cellardyke gene-pool has spread, and it is even more remarkable that so many of us in the twenty-first century are busily researching our "Dyker" roots. For all of us, George Gourlay's Fisher Life; or, The Memorials of Cellardyke and the Fife Coast, better known simply as Fisher Life, is the ultimate source book and bible.

I read Gourlay's book first in my schooldays, when, as a dedicated bookworm, I was reading my way through the entire stock of the Murray Library in Anstruther. Some twenty years later, when I had begun to research my family-tree, I returned to Fisher Life, and was able to identify some of its protagonists as my own forebears. From copying out choice passages from Gourlay's book, I graduated to writing my own history of Cellardyke, and thus Kilrenny and Cellardyke: 800 Years of History (1986) was born. Without George Gourlay's colourful narrative of our ancestors' lives, my own book would have been a much poorer, drier affair.

Fisher Life appeared in 1879, and was only the first of George Gourlay's three books, the others being Our Old Neighbours; or, Folk Lore of the East of Fife (1887) and Anstruther; or, Illustrations of Scottish Burgh Life (1888). It could almost be said that Gourlay was born to write these books, given his early upbringing. His father Andrew Gourlay was a bookseller and bookbinder in Anstruther, but his shop also served as the news and gossip centre of the town, and probably more salty yarns than books were retailed there. In the Preface to Anstruther, George recalled: "I was associated with the bookseller's shop when it was still the news or coffee room, in which the neighbours came far and near to discuss the events of the day. How the silver-haired fathers liked to dwell on the bright world of their youth."

Andrew Gourlay was a farm-labourer's son who had gone to school at Dunino, near St. Andrews, where he was fortunate enough to be taught by the Anstruther poet and scholar William Tennant. Tennant, a classic "lad o' pairts" himself, acted as a talent-spotter for his friend, the Anstruther bookseller William Cockburn, who had published Tennant's comic epic "Anster Fair" with great success, and who was always on the lookout for a promising new apprentice.

The young Andrew Gourlay must have fitted the bill, for at the age of barely 11 he found himself following in the footsteps of another local lad, Archibald Constable - future publisher of Sir Walter Scott and the Encyclopaedia Britannica - to what the author of the Goodsir MS in the National Library of Scotland recalled as 'the low-ceiled Russia and Morocco smelling shop of Mr. Cockburn' at the present 11 Shore Street, Anstruther. Here, "after the battle of Waterloo and the subsequent peace", there gravitated "more than one Admiral and sundry Post-Captains, with not a few straight-backed erect Militaires", and here they "talked of the slow coming news of the day", and relived the great days of their prime. In time the Gourlays, father and son, would continue this tradition of hospitality in their own respective premises, for after serving an apprenticeship with his father, George would open his own shop in Anstruther where he was ably assisted, and after his death succeeded, by his wife Elizabeth Ronald.

George Gourlay's mother Margaret Jack was a native of Pittenweem, and the sister of John Jack, master of the "adventure school" in St. Monans and author of An Historical Account of St Monance, Fifeshire, Ancient and Modern, interspersed with a variety of Tales Incidental, Legendary and Traditional. It is an interesting coincidence that the histories of two East Neuk burghs should have been written by an uncle and nephew, neither of them a native of the village in question.

Gourlay's obituary in the East of Fife Record also tells us that he resembled his uncle Mr. Jac
in having "a very fluent way of speaking in conversation."

If George Gourlay's literary and conversational talents came from the Jack side of his family, th
same could probably be said of a more troublesome inheritance. As a young man Mr. Jack ha
been prevented by defective eyesight from going to sea, and the same affliction governed the live
of his nephews Andrew and George Gourlay. Andrew, brother of George, kept a school at th
Braehead (now West Forth Street) in Cellardyke, where his unfeeling charges would lay obstacle
in his way in hopes that he would fall over them. George, however, found a way of compensatin
for his condition, as his obituarist recalled:

" ... a defect in his eyes, from which he suffered all his life, imposed upon him the task of trustin
to his memory for information. He was highly gifted in this respect, for he had one of the mos
retentive memories any one could possibly wish. He seemed to have the faculty of rememberin
everything he ever heard, and was never behind with dates or figures relating to the past. As a bo
he was a keen listener to the stories and recitals that used to be told in his father's shop, and wha
he then heard he remembered very vividly afterwards." (East of Fife Record, August 28, 1891

We are further informed that he dictated his "numerous articles and paragraphs", clear evidenc
that he found the act of writing difficult. Whether it was his wife or a dedicated friend who acte
as his amanuensis, we are not told.

The vividness of Gourlay's anecdotes is due in large part to the racy dialogue with which they ar
embellished, with names and dates supplied to lend verisimilitude. Often these are linked to som
exploit which led to a new type of fishery, or some successful business venture. An example occur
at the beginning of Chapter 12, when old Alexander Cunningham of the "Box Harry" propose
shooting their nets close to the shore, and despite the scorn of the younger generation ('Just as wee
dae that, faither, in Renny Hill park!), the nets come back full of herring, and the "winter drave
in the Firth of Forth has just been born; causing the exultant paterfamilias to cry to a crewma
"Clash them in the lubber's chafts, Tam!"

The next paragraph describes, with dialogue supplied, Andrew Innes's bold decision to buy fort
barrels of herring and send them to Billingsgate as bloaters - to the consternation of his mast
Bailie George Darsie. "A foolish thing, Andrew, man; a foolish thing", cried the despairing baili
only to turn "radiant as a May morning" when the bloaters realised forty-seven shillings a barre
And lest we are tempted to doubt Gourlay's evidence for all this, he smugly informs us that "th
herrings were bought on the 9th of February 1827."

Nowhere is Gourlay more informative than in his many accounts of disasters at sea, which typicall
are accompanied by dates and names of the victims, with their ages and marital status. It is highl
unlikely that even his prodigious memory could retain such a mass of detail, and it has bee
suggested that he religiously hoarded back numbers of local news-sheet the Pittenweem Regist
and its successor, the East of Fife Record. There is also evidence in "Fisher Life" that he may eve
have interviewed local people and noted down their recollections of events long ago.

In Chapter Eight, "The Wrecks at Cellardyke Harbour", describing the loss of a boat near th
harbour entrance in February1800, when the sole survivor was William "Water Willie" Watson (th
present writer's great-great-great-grandfather), he writes: "I see't the noo," said an eye witnes
hiding her face over the terrible scene of her girlhood, sixty years before, but fresh and vivid a
of yesterday. "The cry's in my lug yet," wept another after a still longer interval ..." This sound
very much like interviews carried out by Gourlay himself, although the first one seems to hav
taken place nearly twenty years before the publication of "Fisher Life". We know that his book
were preceded by a number of articles submitted to a variety of publications, and it was the succes
of these occasional pieces that persuaded him that a book might be a viable proposition. One sense
that his collecting of local lore was a lifelong hobby, rather than a belated attempt to gather dat
when a book was in the offing.

In the latter part of the book no fewer than twenty-four pages are devoted to the terrible losses sustained by the Cellardyke and St. Monans fishing-fleets in the gales of 1875, while engaged in the "south fishing" off East Anglia. This section of the book is a tour de force, as Gourlay gives a blow by blow account of sinkings and narrow escapes, fleshed out by extracts from letters, newspapers and a skipper's log. It is hard to believe that the author was not there to witness these scenes in person.

It would be wrong, however, to suggest that Gourlay was merely an anecdotalist. "Fisher Life" opens with learned citations of Horestii hunters, King James IV, Bishop Kennedy of St. Andrews, and the monks of Balmerino, before he moves on to quote from early burgh charters and council records, many of them now lost. Gourlay had access to these invaluable historical sources in the very building that housed his bookshop, on the corner of High Street and Rodger Street, Anstruther, for the town clerk Matthew Conolly had moved the town clerk's office to the upper floor of that building in 1856, and evidently he afforded his friend Mr.Gourlay free access to the records of which he was the custodian. This proved particularly useful when Gourlay was working on his last and most ambitious book, "Anstruther", which brought him wide acclaim, including an appreciative postcard from Prime Minister W. G. Gladstone.

George Gourlay died of a lung inflammation on 26th August, 1891, at the early age of fifty-nine. He was survived by his wife, a daughter and three sons, one of whom became a well-known journalist and the first editor of the "Leven Mail".

The reappearance of Gourlay's "Fisher Life" is good news for anyone with an interest in Scottish local history, and in particular the history of our fishing communities. Those who have sought it in libraries over the years, and photocopied favourite passages, will be delighted to have their own copy at last. Those who have only heard of it, and looked in vain for a copy, have a rare treat in store. All of us owe a debt of gratitude to the Fife Family History Society for giving it back to us in this handsome format.

Harry D. Watson
Edinburgh, 12th December 2003

Fisher Life; or The Memorials of Cellardyke and The Fife Coast. By George Gourlay

First published 1879 by John Innes, Cupar

Second edition (with foreword by Harry D Watson), published 2004 by
The Fife Family History Society

ISBN 0 9531443 1 3

ACKOWLEDGMENTS

Harry D Watson, the author of Kilrenny and Cellardyke: 800 Years of History, for writing
the foreword.

Eric Eunson and Stenlake Publishing for the cover photographs of Cellardyke Harbour
(1905) and Mrs Elizabeth Gourlay

Printed by Levenmouth Printers, Toll Park, Station Road, Muiredge, Buckhaven,
Fife KY8 1JH (Tel: 01592 715531)

FISHER LIFE;

OR, THE

MEMORIALS OF CELLARDYKE

AND THE

FIFE COAST.

BY

GEORGE GOURLAY,

ANSTRUTHER.

CUPAR: "FIFE HERALD" OFFICE.
ANSTRUTHER: GEORGE GOURLAY, BOOKSELLER.
1879.

CUPAR-FIFE: PRINTED IN THE "FIFE HERALD" AND "FIFE NEWS" OFFICE.

CONTENTS.

CHAPTER XI.

CHAPTER XII.

CHAPTER XIII.

CHAPTER XIV.

THE MONKS

FISHERMEN.

CHAPTER I.

INTRODUCTION.

One day, perchance, an Horestii hunter, wandering as the
child of Nature by sea and shore, stops to pile or dig his hut
by the brink of the skerrie, where he can launch his skiff or
coracle, or chase the wild boar in the adjacent woods. The
incident is scarcely more than the print of his naked foot
upon the sands, but it is the birth-day, according to some of
the fisher homes of Fife, those picturesque little seaports,
ringing ever since with the melody of life and love. If, however, the conjecture is true concerning Skinfasthaven, or
Cellardyke, and a hamlet had really sprung up at the little
creek, it lay unnoticed and unknown in the eye of history till
the eventful day when the lands of Kilrenny passed, by the gift
of the unfortunate James the Third, into the hands of his
kinsman, James Kennedy, the last and greatest of the Bishops
of St Andrews. This was in 1452, and the change is immediately
signalised, if we believe the old fathers, by the erection of the
" Bishop's House," a stately tenement built, like the grange
house of an old abbey, on a tier of massive arches, and shielded

by the pier, which was originally designed, they also tell us, to save it from the storm. We look back at this point through the mist of more than four centuries; but nevertheless the Bishop and his undertaking can be traced with singular precision amongst the shadows. But let us glance for a little at the romantic circumstances of the times. Thus going no further than Anstruther, on the opposite side of the brook, the Monks of Balmerino are seen so extensively concerned with the enterprise of the deep that the famous baptistry of St Ayles is reserved for their own sea folk, and only a mile or two further on, the beach of Pittenweem and St Monance is ringing with the sailor's song, as the big ship, gunwale deep with pickled cod or herrings, and with the Prior's flag at the main, sails out in the breeze, her course for France or Spain, from which she will not return till her freight has been exchanged for the silks and wines of those sunny lands. " Here is the secret of the golden fringe to the begger's mantle," or the old world wealth of the Fifeshire coast—a secret which none knew better than Bishop Kennedy; and remembering what the historian tells us of his great ship that was the greatest in the seas, of his princely freights that yet live in the crowning splendours of the ancient city, we can so far see and understand his work on our kindly shore, where he could participate in the harvest as he and his predecessors had never done, or could do, on the stormy bay of St Andrews.

After his death the succeeding Archbishops saw it to be their interest to continue to be the same kind masters to the little colony, which one day under them rose to the dignity and consequence of a burgh of regality. It was to the lasting envy of the fishing village of East Anstruther; but a great change was soon to follow, as we find that about seventeen years before the Reformation the lands and port of Kilrenny had ceased to belong to the Church, having been disposed of by Cardinal Bethune to his favourite cousin John, who at the same time bought the vicarage or fish teinds of the Barony from the Monks of Dryburgh, to whom, with the Parish Church, they had been given as a gift to God by the Countess Ada, the mother of Malcolm the Maiden and William the Lion, those royal brothers, so strangely different in their character and history. The purchase of the teinds, however, deserves more than a passing notice. It is, in fact, one of the most memorable transactions of the period in a local point of view, for the fish teinds of Anstruther, having at the same time passed into the hands of the knight of Dreel, a yet existing agreement was concluded between the two friends, according to which their vassals were to have a mutual right to the harbours, but without any compromise in the case of the teinds, which every vassal was to pay to his own laird, or, in other words, the Skimfie fisher had no taxmaster at Anstruther pier except Laird Bethune for the teinds, and so it fared in like manner with the Anstruther fishers when they sailed into Skimfie, as the old world called the little creek of Skinfasthaven.

CHAPTER II.

THE OLD RECORDS AND FISHER LIFE.

" The wrath of heaven is on sea and shore," exclaimed the old friar when his nest had been blown down in the storm which overturned the Church of Rome at the Reformation, and his finger, as he did so, was pointed at one of those sea famines, which have so often come and gone in the story of the shore. But the tide turns at last, and thus before the end of the century the fisheries had so recovered that the Bailies of Kilrenny were able to rebuild and improve their harbour so as to anticipate, like their neighbours, a new and brighter era for the coast. We are indebted for this interesting fact to the old records, which at this time contain many curious glimpses into the fisher life of three centuries ago. Thus we learn from the archives of Crail that it was the established custom to have an indentured apprenticeship in the fisher boat, at the expiry of which the master or his widow was bound to fit out the young mariner with a net and line as the " sea-going gear " of the period. An old burgh charter, of date 1580, gives a valuable hint, for by it the Laird of Anstruther stipulates for 200 herrings " for ilk drave boat in my said town labouring at the winter draves yearly, and for ilk boat passing to the lanthrang lines, within the Scot's Frith, a kylling and a bannock fluke yearly and ilk year if the same be gotten "—that is, every boat at the great lines during the season in Lent was to give a cod and a turbot, the " Scot's Frith " or sea being the ancient name for the Firth of Forth.

Creers, as the large half-decked boats, rigged with mainmast and mizen, were called, now sailed from every East Neuk harbour to fish herrings at the Lewis, or perhaps cod and ling at the Orkney Isles; but while ploughing in distant seas the old fishers did not forget their native shore, which, in the eyes of the Hollander at least, was the " treasure house" of Scotland. And the idea does not end here, for just as the Australian digger writes home that the revolver must be as ready to his hand as the pickaxe or the shovel, so the fishers of Fife had then to face other storms than those of the midnight wave. The Dutch were the undisputed masters of the open sea; but any herring day, Mynheer, vaunting in his big 'bus, which floated like a tower amongst the boats, would sweep into the Auld Haikes or the Traith, from which he would only be beaten, if beaten at all, by cutlass and pike; but there were other adversaries to fight, and those much nearer the doors. It is a curious characteristic of the times, that the merchants of Cupar and St Andrews, and even Dundee, would come marching across the hills armed to the teeth, though on no more hostile errand than to buy and cure herring like their neighbours of the coast. In doing so, however, they forgot, or rather defied, the jealous laws, and still more jealous spirit of the burghs, and the intruders were at once resisted as pirates and robbers. A hundred times and more the Billowness and the Golden Strand have rung with the strife of tongues, and the noise of sterner battle; but as year by year saw the strangers in greater force an appeal was taken, as we gather again and again from the records, to the Convention of Royal Burghs, but at the very instant when all parties were hotest in the controversy the cause and the quarrel disappeared with the herring from the Forth.

CHAPTER III.

TWO CENTURIES AGO.

At this period the story of the coast becomes like a sad and weary prospect, in which the landmarks are all calamity and woe. Turning away from greater misfortunes we need only refer to an entry by old Clerk Spalding, which runs as follows :—

"1642.—Up to this time, from the beginning of the year, there was a scarcity of white fish along the east coast, and to the hurt and hunger of the poor and beggaring of the fishermen. It was reported that when the fishers had laid their lines and taken fishes abundantly there came ane beast, called the sea dog, to the lines, and ate and destroyed the haill bodies, and left nothing on the lines but the heads. A judgment surely from God Almighty, for the like scarcity of fishes to continue so long has scarcely been seen here in Scotland, whilk bred great dearth of meal and malt at aucht, nine, or ten pounds the boll, and all other meats also very dear." Our own gossiping Fife chronicler, John Lamont, in the parish of Largo, continues the doleful story in his famous diary thus :— "1658 as also 1657.—Thir two yeares ther was few or no herring gotten in Fyfe syde, and not many in Dunbar, so that divers persons beganne to feare ther sould be no drewe hereafter, which was a great prejudice to the poor fisher men, as also to the whole places nereabout (for the like had not beine, as some thinke, for the space of a hundred years before.) 1662 and 1663.—Ther was no herring gotten in like manner." But one pleasing anecdote invites remembrance. It is told in this way :—" In the eventful times when Episcopacy had been established in Scotland under the primacy of James Sharp, sometime minister of Crail, Robert Bennet was the incumbent of Kilrenny, a man of strong Covenanting sentiments, but who, being of an exceedingly mild and retiring character, stood for a time irresolute in the great crisis around him. One day, while his mind was much agitated about what course he should pursue, he went down amongst his fisher parishioners of Cellardyke. It was the morning after a great sea storm that had overthrown the pier, and the people were all striving with might and main to raise a bulwark against the upflowing tide, none being more busily employed in carrying stones than the widow of a fisherman that had been drowned some years before. The good minister stood for a time intently watching the scene, and then drew near the spot, accosting the widow, as he did so with the question how she came to be so employed. ' I'm helpin', as you see, sir, for the bairns, they'll aiblins be the better o' it.' The incident made its own impression on the sensitive mind of Robert Bennet, who turned away. ' There was a poor fisherwoman faithful to her duty as she saw it in the light of a mere earthly affection, while he, " an appointed leader of the Church, wavered and stood irresolute when the Master's cause was being betrayed, and the flock led away to the desert." ' ' He felt ashamed,' he tells us, ' his conscience upbraided him,' and from that day he gave that clear and emphatic testimony for Presbytery, which although it speedily led to his being expelled from the Church of Kilrenny, yet secured for him a place amongst the heroes of his time."

Here the public records again become the guides of our narrative, but the minutes are as sad, if not sadder than before. Cellardyke, like the other sea towns of Fife, had been sinking for years, in the distress of the times, till in the crisis of her misfortunes in 1672, the Bailies presented a supplication to the Scottish Parliament, praying to be relieved from sending a member or Commissioner, who was then paid, like any other delegate, for his services. The Bailies asserted at this time, what Laird Bethune repeated at the Union, that the town had never possessed a royal charter, that the rights so long exercised as by such were only assumed and unchallenged, but now the petitioners prayed for restoration to their own proper, if humbler, place as a burgh of regality. This supplication was also supported by a touching account of the sufferings of the town, and became the subject of a long and tedious investigation, but being again and again renewed more urgently than before, it was at last sustained, and Kilrenny was ordered to be expunged from the rolls of Parliament as a royal burgh; but as it is well known the decree, like the process, began and ended with the disastrous era.

CHAPTER IV.

BETTER TIMES.

More than two generations, indeed, were thus as one long and dismal night to the shores of Fife; but daybreak came at last. The watchers, however, were faint and weary, and it came so suddenly that the glorious event—we refer to the Revolution—was like the risen sun, before it was known to many an honest burgher by land and sea. The first public messenger, indeed, was the Kilrenny weaver, running out of the conventicle to ring the joyful news long and loud in the old steeple, and the veteran skipper, fined till he lost his brig for his share in the escape of the Covenant saint across the seas, who that same evening hoists the old ensign as the flag of victory, which, as it streams in the breeze, is seen and rejoiced over by every faithful eye upon the shore.

Such, according to tradition, was the jubilee day over the great historical event which was in truth the advent of a happier future. But let the burgh records tell their other aspect of the story.

Thus in 1691, at the rouping of the anchorages and shore dues, old William Donaldson appeared at "the running of the glass," as the entry goes, and became the tacksman at his own offer of £34 Scots; but in 1703 the prosperous fishery had raised the same common good to £73 Scots.

As in the beginning of the century strangers flocked from other shores "to work the silver mine;" but the Bailies of those days had an iron grasp for such intruders, and so we learn that in February 1693 they adjudge in a Burgh Court Alexander Murray, William Doig, John Donaldson, each of them shall pay a dollar for the unfree trading, and packing, and selling of fish, and ordains them to remain in ward until they pay their fines.   Every picture has its own shadow, and a dark one at this time falls on the fisher homes of Cellardyke. The old mothers weep, " Trouble rise to poor folk oot o' the ground," but we leave our readers to Clerk Cunningham's minute of date 30th May 1693.   The said day the Bailies and Council of this burgh made report of the Act of Parliament made for levying of seamen, and of their putting out of five fishermen for this burgh, who were kept in prison ten days before they were sent away, and that the expense of keeping and *reacking* out these men will amount to £72, paid by the Treasurer.   The Bailies and Council think it best to write to Alexander Stevenson, their Commissioner, and George Bethune, that he may apply to Parliament to see if any restitution can be had until the £72 be paid.

Here is a graphic peep at the herring successes of a hundred and seventy years ago :—

Kilrenny, 3d September 1701.—The said day the Bailies and Council, for avoiding any disorder and confusion that arises amongst those men in this burgh in the time of delivering herring by running all to one or two boats or to strangers, and neglecting to unload the boats belonging to other burgesses in the meantime, for removing whereof the Bailies and Council statute and ordain, in time coming, when the boats come in with herring, and are to unload, that the horsemen shall divide themselves equally amongst the boats that every burgess may be served alike, and discharges them to serve any stranger until the burgesses and inhabitants be served, and the boats of burgesses unloaded, and ordains all persons contravening the said statute shall be convicted in a fine of £1 Scots to the public use.

The following extract is at least curious and suggestive :—

Here we see that the brand and branding fee are no new thing in Scotland (Kilrenny, 4th September 1707.)   The said Bailies and Council, in obedience to the late Act of Parliament, made anent the herring and salmon fishing, appoints Andrew Gooland, Councillor burgess of this burgh, as visitor, and John Gooland, cooper, his brother, to visit all the herrings and casks to be exported out of this burgh this present year, and if they find the same sufficient to mark them with the town's mark and visitor's mark ; and if insufficient to seize upon the same, conform to Act of Parliament, and to do everything requisite thereanent conform to the Act of Council, made thereanent the last year, who, having compeared personally before the said Bailies and Council, accepted of the respective offices in and upon them, and gave their oaths *de fideli administratione ;* and they are hereby empowered to exact for their pains from the owners of the herrings so to be visited and marked the sum allowed for each cask of said herrings and cask allowed by the foresaid Act of Parliament, which was acted.

CHAPTER V.

THE JACOBITES AND THE FISHERMEN, &c.

In these years we obtain some valuable details of the fishery from Sir Robert Sibbald, who visited the coast in connection with his famous " History of Fife." The information refers to the year 1710, when he writes :—" St Monance hath usually ten fishing boats, with four men in each ; but during the herring fishing (which is in August) they send out twelve boats, and seven men in each and sometimes more." In his description of the sister port he says :—" The lower part of the town of Pittenweem lieth alongst their two havens. The west haven is near the panns, and fit only for fish boats. Of late they had only six fishing boats, with six men in each, and they had fifteen boats for the fishing of herring, with seven men in each, but now more." East Anstruther was yet full of the spirit of Fisher Willie, for he says concerning the town's folk :—" They have good magazines and cellars for trade, and are provided with all accommodations for making and curing of herring, and which is the staple commodity of this town, and of all the towns in the east coast of Fife. And this town sends about twenty-four boats to the fishing of herring. Formerly they sent yearly about thirty boats to the fishing of herring at Lewis." Cellardyke is thus referred to :—" It consists of one street, and hath ten boats, with six men in each, that fish all the year over for white fish, but in the season for fishing herring they set out twenty, with seven men in each. It hath a little harbour." Thus much of the fishing, but the crews now described by Sir Robert had occasionally other adventures than with net and line. For instance, we find them busy, as a labour of love, at the erection of the breakwater in Anstruther sands, built but thrown down by the first storm, within a year or two of his visit. That was a more eventful night, however, when the Cellardyke fishers gave a passage in these boats to Brigadier Mackintosh, the old Borlam of unforgotten terrors, and his Highlanders, though under the guns of the King's ships in the memorable rising of 1715. The laird and his drunken cronie, Dominie Robert Wilson, were the only Jacobites in the parish ; but the fishers, so distinguished for their loyalty and patriotism in all genera- tions, were enlisted for one night at least in their plots, less, however, by the silver bribe than by the terrible oath of the gallows looking captain, who vowed to take the boats and fire the town if the skippers were not ready to his signal. The burgh records here waken into romance :—

Kilrenny, 5th March 1716.—Council met. Sederunt— James Peacock, Thomas Waddell, David Ramsay, Bailie James Waid, treasurer ; William Pitbladdo, Stephen William- son, David Lowson, William Craigie, James Davidson, William Arnot, Andrew Murray, David Reid, Councillors. The Bailies laid before the Council a letter come to their hands from the Provost of Edinburgh, calling a meeting and Convention of the Burghs, with respect to the burdens they have of late lain under, and the invasion and encroachments upon our privileges, and the great decay of trade amongst us, so that this exceed- ingly imports us to deliberate upon the proper remedy. This letter is dated 16th February last.

They nominated and chose Captain Alexander Stevenson, merchant in Edinburgh, their burgess, and who had formerly represented this Burgh in the Scots Parliament and the burghs, to be their Commissioner, and his commission to be given him by way of extract, and ordains an account to be sent of the cess or contribution the Earl of Mar imposed, and of them, which was £3 3s sterling, and the treasurer to draw out the account due to the several burgesses and inhabitants by the Highland armies they owe for meat and drink and otherwise at their transporting from this side to North Berwick or south side, and this beside £20 sterling promised to each boat of six who were forced over with them, and never paid.

The fishermen never obtained redress, but their home comforts were not resting at the time on such rewards. Fisher life, it is true, has ever the echo which rings to us from the Sea of Galilee, when "they toiled all night and caught nothing," or when they cried in the crash of the tempest, " Help, Lord, or we perish ;" but yet when they remembered the old stories told by the evening fire, Cellardyke that day had much, very much, to be thankful for. The herring, perhaps, had as many vagaries as ever, but the haddock and the cod were true to the old haunts, and so abundant that the following singular facts are on record by the well-known minister of Kilrenny, William Beat, who was the son of a Bailie in Cellardyke, where he was born about 1710 :—He remembers, he tells us, when the mackerel was fished with success at the doors, and as for the cod and the ling, he has seen some ten or twelve big boats sailing into the harbour loaded to the gunwale, and with perhaps thirty or forty, or even fifty, of the largest cod fastened to a rope and towed at the stern. Nor was this all. As many as fifty boats, with six men each, launched out to the drave, as part of the great fleet then casting their nets on the Lammas sea, so great, indeed, that like the trees of the forest, he could not number them, though he has heard it said the collector at Anstruther, whose duty it was to do so, estimated them as not less than 500—this collector, by the way, being no other than

Alexander Macnaughton, who instituted the famous or rather infamous order of the sovereign and knights of the Beggar's Benison. The merchant prince of those days was Robert Fall in Dunbar, who had the biggest cod on the Fife side all the year through at 4d the piece, always subject, however, to the old burgh law, by which the inhabitants had the right to go to the bulwark and "kitchen the barley bannock" with the best fish at their own price. "What, at their own price?" echoes a friend, and of course people never paid more than the merchant's fee, or, as the venerable minister assures us, of the very finest of the "many thousands" sold under his own eye he never knew any to sell at more than a groat. The old pastor lived to see the great sea famine of the Forth, when the golden past rose so vividly before him that he goes on to tell that, incredible as it might be, he himself had seen the luxury, as it was now esteemed, of a "cod head" lying in heaps amongst the offal that manured the fields.

To complete the picture of those lucky times, he goes on to say that the fishers salted their winter beef at a "merk" the stone, or less than a penny a pound ; that the fat hen of the wedding feast cost only the price of a cod or a fourpenny bit ; and further, that the housewife spread the oaten cake, or "soomed St Peter's fish," with butter at threepence the pound.

But we turn from the manse, though as we do so it is our good fortune to be introduced to the worthy fishers themselves. Here is the story—

"In 1755 the town of East Anstruther was very much involved in debt, owing partly to the erection a few years before of the present west pier, but much more to the feasting and carousing in which the Council indulged while managing, or rather mismanaging, the municipal affairs. All fishing boats, with the exception of those of Cellardyke, regularly paid teinds for the fish and herrings they might land at Anstruther harbour—the teinds being let to a tacksman in the same way as the customs of the burgh. The Cellardyke boats had always been exempt, and a dim idea prevailed that they were so in virtue of an ancient charter, but, as that charter was thought to be no longer in existence, the Anstruther Bailies resolved that the privilege should be forthwith challenged, and the Cellardyke boats made to pay like their neighbours, and, as the herring fishing had revived on the coast, a considerable addition to the revenue of the burgh was thus anticipated. Accordingly, at the next letting of the teinds, a hard-fisted cooper, named James M'Dougal, the father of the eccentric worthy of the same name, became their tacksman on the understanding that the Magistrates would support him in his claims on the Cellardyke men. The fishers on their part threatened to stand out to the uttermost, but next year, at least, it was likely there would be no occasion for any dispute upon the matter, as the herring fishing had proved for several weeks a complete failure. Towards the end of September, however, a shoal of herrings set in off the Billowness, when eleven Cellardyke boats came into Anstruther with a total of 190 crans on the 18th, and with 94 and 120 crans respectively on the two following days. The poor fishers were instantly pounced upon by the surly cooper, that played the part of Friday to 'greedy' Treasurer James Johnston, of East Anstruther, who demanded teind at the rate of 1s per pound from all and sundry—the herrings having, as was usual at that time, been sold by the count at 1s per 100 on the first and second days, and at 1s 4d on the third. The skippers, as one of their wives, strapping Kirsty Powrie said, 'wudna' allow ony Bailie in Anstruther to mak' a hole in their bairnies' parritch caup,' and so they stoutly refused to pay the iniquitous demand, whereupon they were each and all summoned to appear in Court at Anstruther on the 24th October, before the Admiral of Fife, who then had jurisdiction in such cases. It was a memorable day in Cellardyke the holding of that Court, the eleven defenders—James Watt, William Powrie, Thomas Watson, James Miller, William Dryburgh, Thomas Scott, John Anderson, Andrew Boyter, Robert Anderson, George Lothian, and William Young, with all the fishers and most of the wives of Cellardyke, were in due time at the old Tolbooth of East Anstruther—then a little grim, low-roofed apartment, which could not have held a tenth of the great crowd that pressed against the huge oaken door. The case was thought to be already tried and lost for the poor fishers, for by a reputed intrigue John Cunningham, the Anstruther clerk, a chosen friend of Bailie Johnston's, was to sit as Admiral Substitute, and so when this judge, who was a tall, thin man, with stooping shoulders, came upon the scene, there was a colour of truth in the bitter remark of an outspoken fisherwife, 'that gin he looted, it wasna' that justice burthened his back.' The Magistrates and Councillors, with crafty Bailie Johnston of Pitkierie at their head, marched in great state to the Court-Room, when, with all the formality of a little brief authority, the judge assumed his functions. The cases were then called, when, in vindication of the plea, Treasurer Johnston stood up, and in a thick and husky voice, but all the more so on this occasion from the effects of smuggled gin, read, or attempted to read, an old charter granted by Colin Adam, minister of Kilrenny, and vicar of the Parish Church there, on the 28th September 1636, in which he surrendered to the Town Council of East Anstruther the teinds of all fish landed at the harbour, so far as these belonged to the vicarage of Kilrenny.

B

" This was considered to be unanswerable proof, and with a haughty look, Judge Cunningham demanded of the defenders 'how they dared to dispute so just a claim ?'

" The skippers were all silent ; there was not a man of them but had faced the Storm King in his wildest moods without a passing fear, but somehow or other the hardy fellows looked awkward and confused as they stood at the bar of the ricketty old Court-Room. After a brief pause, however, little Skipper Miller stepped to the front, and in his own blunt way stated that he and George Lothian had been all the road to Balfour House to see their Laird, Mr Henry Bethune, who had told them that the Anstruther Bailies were a set of reiving loons, as he (the Laird) could prove by papers in his charter chest, which his man of business would look for, and send to Cellardyke without delay. The little skipper concluded by craving that the Court might be adjourned until these documents could be produced.

" The Laird of Balfour was not a man to be trifled with, and so the Court was adjourned until that day three weeks, but Bailie Johnston could not conceal his annoyance ; and, turning to the Judge, he exclaimed, in spiteful allusion to the coarse jacket of the poor fisher, ' that he hoped Mr Bethune would not only be able to give his mandatory a charter, but a coat also by the next Court ;' whereupon all the Bailies and Coun-cillors, and Judge Cunningham, held their sides and laughed outright at the wit of the first Magistrate of Anstruther. On the day appointed the Court again met, when, to the great consternation of the Anstruther authorities, Skipper Miller drew from the inside pocket of his rough sea jacket a roll of parchment, which, on being examined, proved to be the charter obtained in 1543 by John Bethune, which, as we have already stated, clearly exonerated the Cellardyke boats from all teinds but those leviable by the Lairds of Kilrenny.

" The tables were now completely turned, and without a single word the Bailies quietly left the Court. The Judge, however, to please his friends as far as possible pretended to question the authenticity of the document, and again adjourned the Court. The case, however, was virtually settled, and when the skippers appeared for a third time in the Tolbooth, it was to be formally absolved from the suit, and thus ended, to the signal disgrace of the Anstruther Bailies, their famous persecution of the fishermen."

CHAPTER VI.

SEA LIFE A HUNDRED YEARS AGO.

It is then that the traveller, in a visit to the East of Fife, sees the tall houses, the malt kilns and stores on the Braehead of Cellardyke, with the hundred wine cellars and gin magazines elsewhere, fast sinking into roofless and dingy ruins. The square-rigged ships thronging the harbours, till they looked like a forest, with topgallant and royal mast; the sledge trains rumbling along the causeways, till they appeared almost alive with bag and barrel, had all disappeared as the sunshine of yesterday in the shadow of the Union, or the odious taxes which had followed. Neither dynasty nor Government, however, could rob the coast of heaven's own gift in the fisheries, which, amid all changes, continued on the whole to prosper. It is a suggestive fact that the patriarch, James Nairn, who died in 1771, added £55 to his stipend from the herring teinds of East Anstruther; but here is the testimony of an eye witness concerning the coast of 1778, or one hundred years ago. It is the public-spirited inspector of the fisheries, David Loch, who says of Cellardyke—"A good fishing is carried on here. The people are very industrious." He had a Fife side tour on the first Saturday of August, and continues—"There are at present in Crail eleven boats on the herring fishing, about fifteen at Cellardyke, four at Pittenweem, and nearly the same number of small yawls on the white fishing. On Monday, the 7th, I visited the fishers and all concerned in the fishing trade, who were in high spirits on account of their success, very considerable quantities of herrings having been taken. Thirteen boats are employed

on the herring fishing at St Monance, and about the same
number of small boats ply the white fishing on this coast.
The people here being very industrious, are all become wealthy
by their trade and fishing." Mr Loch is very interested about
the great herring kilns on the south side, and goes on—" It is
to be observed that none of the inhabitants on the coast of
Fife from Fifeness to St Monance have yet begun to redden
herrings." They, however, understood, and were about to
begin the romantic process according to this patriot, who
adds, " No less a sum than two thousand pounds sterling has
been received by the above fishers for herrings sold to the
country people for their own use, and to others for salting as
white herrings, who sent them up the Firth to supply those
who inhabit the populous banks of the Forth, so that this
lucrative trade on the two sides of the Firth has brought into
this spot of our country within a few weeks eight thousand
five hundred pounds sterling of a clear gain all by labour."

In conclusion Mr Loch deals with the great fisher grievance
of that day. It is in reference to the Admiral's Court, which
we saw in the teind case was held in Anstruther, though it
also frequently sat in Cellardyke and the sister towns ; but to
take his own words—" The Honourable James Wemyss of
Wemyss, deputy-admiral of the fishing over all the coast of
Fife, has, I think, very improperly fixed his substitute at
Dysart, at which place all the Courts on the fishing affairs on
the East Coast of Fife are holden and litigations or disputes
determined. Dysart being full twenty miles from the fishing
towns on the coast, where herrings commonly, I had almost said
always, set in, the poor fishermen are obliged to trudge that
distance to attend the Court, or suffer decreet to pass against
them in absence." This was the fate of the St Monance fishermen, of whom no less than six boats' crews must have remained

idle for two days in the harvest of fishing to go twenty miles
to attend Mr Wemyss' Court.

And so for the next eleven or twelve years life on the coast
continued—that is, with a certain fulness in basket and store;
but a calamity is at hand, which, as we shall see, is to bring
hunger and hardship to every home.   It is the great haddock
famine—the seven years' dearth of the old fisher—which was
perhaps the more overwhelming, because, like the midnight
storm, all eyes were closed, till ruin and misery were written
around them.   A curious story, it is true, had come up from
the Buchan coast.   It was about a terrible sea monster, having,
as the tale ran, a head big as a drave boat, covered with
bristles, grey in colour, but long and shaggy as the tangles on
the skerry; that with the size of the whale it had the swift-
ness and ferocity of the shark ; at least so it seemed to the
poor northern crew, who saw a single toss of that dreadful
tale brush away their fishing tackle with as little effort as the
strong wing cleaves the gossamer ; but the disasters did not
end with the day, for ever since the haddock, as if sharing the
terror of man, had fled from the invaded seas.   " It was only
the brig capsized in the gale," growled the old boatswain ; "it
was all smuggled gin," snivelled the spiteful cobbler; "it must
be the kracken," said the novel reading fisher lass, Annie
Watson, the mother of the one day Professor Tennant ; but the
old fishers only laughed, though they confessed they were no
wiser than their neighbours to tell the secret of the hungry sea.
Still it was the echo in the distance, now rising now falling on
the gale, and perchance but little heeded till that memorable
day, in the early summer of 1790, when the anxious cry rings
on the shore, as boat after boat lands at the bulwark and not
a single haddock, or without " drawin' bluid," to borrow the
sea phrase of the time.   Next day, and next, and next the

lines were cast on opposite tacks, but the home coming was the same, and now the harvest gone trials and troubles soon found an open door. Nothing, however, is so eloquent as the voice of an eye-witness, and here it is from the first statistical account of the Scottish parishes. Going back to the narrow tall-gabled manse, as it abuts on the churchyard wall at Kilrenny, we find the old minister broken with grief for the loss of his cherished partner, " the rare instance of conjugal fidelity," of her tombstone; but he lifts his head over the kindly memories of the past, already before the reader. These, indeed, are all sunshine compared with the gloomy present; the fishery, whether by net or line, a forlorn failure, the haddock especially being to-day a rare stranger, as it had been for the last two years. The little world around him is changed, but it is all for the worse. In 1755 the population of the parish was 1348, but now he ascertains it to be only 1086, owing in part to the growing size of the farms, but far more to the famine of the sea. To-day, he continues, there are but two breweries in Cellardyke, though he could remember the time when there were four-and-twenty; nor is this all, for to increase the public perplexity, provisions are at a ransom price, for he tells us, as things not to be forgotten, of a hen at a shilling, beef at fourpence, and fresh butter at eightpence a pound. We are also indebted to the old Presbyter, William Beat, for the origin of Cellardyke, not, as some say, because the old fishers had their houses at the Kirkton, and their tackle stores or cellars at the beach, but in consequence, he tells us, of the great salt and barrel stores of the herring trade and traders of ancient Skimfie.

Pittenweem shore, however, was still more dreary, for, according to Dr Nairn, while there were seventy-two sailors there were only twelve fishers who manned the five small yawls that swing in the ebb at the west harbour. He mentions, but merely so, the well-known smacks, which at this time touched on the coast in order to run the turbot or "bannock fluke" alive to Billingsgate, an experiment which did not prosper, though for years an English company had two or three well built, well manned cutters afloat in the lobster trade, which yearly, it is said, put over a thousand pounds into the pockets of the East of Fife fishermen.

St Monance, we learn from old Archibald Gillis, sent sixteen drave boats, some with six, and others with as many as nine of a crew; but the fishing was only followed from year's end to year's end by the eighty men, or twenty crews, who plied hook and line in a class of small but trusty yawls, which danced like sea ducks in all weather. The notice refers to 1795, or the "black year," as it is called, when the oatmeal rose to the unprecedented price for the time of 15d the peck. So great, indeed, was the distress, especially amongst the seafaring families, that the Kirk-Session arranged with the "friend of the poor," Sir Robert Anstruther, for the bolls of Balcaskie, by which the "parritch pat" was stirred at 3d the peck under the market price. Crail, however, furnishes the most interesting details. They are by the exact but kindly Andrew Bell, who gives the fishing industry in 1791 at thirteen drave boats, six great line boats, and six smaller ones employed in the lobster fishing. He also gives the number of fishermen at 42 or 44; but though the supplies of cod and ling were still abundant, the haddock had become such a rarity that 4d or 6d was paid for a single fish, when but a few years before they were any day bought at the pier for five halfpence the dozen. The herring fishing, he further says, was on the decline, and the reasons he gives are at least as plausible as many of the conjectures of the present day. He hints, it is true, at the over fishing theory, the "industry of man ruining the shoals," as he says ; but the great enemy, in his eye, was the Dutch, who, with their big 'buses and their drifts, would sweep and gather all before them for miles, and that within two or three leagues from the shore. The minister of Crail, like his brethren by the sea, has a special allusion to the Greenland ships, which had been for years, but more especially after the failure of the fisheries, the grand hope of the Fife coast nigh forty years before, when the rival politicians, Sir John Anstruther and William Alexander, sent out the two big whalers from Anstruther, the one the Hawk and the other the Rising Sun ; many, if not most, of the crews were from Cellardyke. The adventure soon ended in the wreck of the first and the dismantling of the second ship ; but from that day the flower of the shore was more or less on board the whaling fleet, the stout old ships from Dundee or Dunbar or elsewhere, that chased the Greenland whale.

CHAPTER VII.

THE SORROWS OF THE SEA.

Life in every condition has its own lights and shadows, but with none do they come and go so much like the tints of autumn, the sunshine and the storm, as with the toiler on the deep. Where, for instance, is the widow's wail so often heard as when rising on the sea breeze, over the lofty topmast riven on the sands, or the gallant boat whelmed and lost in the angry waves? And these are not the griefs of yesterday, but the old world well knew and sadly wept the sorrows of the sea, though never perhaps so often and so bitterly as we of to-day. Nor if so is the reason far to seek. The ancient fisher was contented with his skiff, however small and rudely fashioned, but then he and his comrades scarcely ventured beyond the shadows of the land, or in such a situation that with ready oar they could escape almost with the first signal of danger on the winter sky. He had, indeed, no barometer or semaphore, but his storm signal jingled constantly in his ear; now in the cry of the sea bird, as in the rhyme—

> "When you hear the burl cry,
>   Let you the boatie lie;
>   Twa ebbs and a flude,
>   Be the weather ere so gude;"

or again, in the boom of the rising east wind on the islet skerries, when

> "The stell begins to knell,
>   An' Pillie begins to route,
>   The Mayman cries unto his boys
>   Turn the boat about."

But still the old fathers did not always escape; as then as now, disaster came : a sudden squall, a split in the plank, sent boat and crew to the bottom.

Thus in 1766 an Earlsferry boat was capsized in a gale, when, of the 18 fishers who dwelt in the old burgh, six met with a watery grave.

A mournful cry arose on the 15th of May 1765 at the shore of Pittenweem over the loss of a haddock fishing boat and eight men ; but it is so far pleasing to add that the widow and the orphan were not forgotten ; in particular the old Parliamenter of the East Neuk burghs, Sir Henry Erskine, who had lodgings in West Anstruther, sent fifteen guineas by way of a Christian gift.

Tradition has much to tell of similar catastrophes at Cellardyke. Grey heads no longer with us would say how, when the midnight sea was shining like silver in the harvest moon, a well-known sail was seen gliding like a spirit towards the shore. Suddenly a black squall, like the shadow of death, sweeps the lovely scene. It comes and goes, but the boat is seen no more. They are swift to the rescue ; but the floating wreck is only left to tell the fishers' fate.

An aged grandsire, passed to the silent land, had a touching story of the sea. Boat after boat had crossed the bar with the ebbing tide, but one crew had clung to the last chance of saving their gear, and night and the storm still saw them out on the raging deep. Few then thought of a pillow in Cellardyke ; even women and children waited and watched till morning on the lonely beach. "See, a boat, a boat !" at last cries one, pointing where, in the eye of day, the little craft comes heading to the shore. It is a terrible moment. Destruction seems to ride on the whirlwind, and death to sit on every billow that rolls and booms on the reefs; but a brave hand is on the rudder, and the boat comes gallantly on. Again and again the crowd, after a long breath, see her rise like a sea bird on the waves, and the danger is lessening fast, when it is but the work of a moment, a wave leaps, like a treacherous enemy, towards the boat.

"She has broached to," rings out like a death cry, and the seas are over the doomed gunwale like the foam on the sunken skerrie. The shadows are still deep on the shore, but the work of death has been done. Already, as if in mockery, float and oar are cast to land. "They're a' drooned!" shrieks a bereaved sister. "I'm saved," a voice seems to answer from the grave, and they turned to find the only survivor of the wreck. This was Alexander Gardiner, one of an old crofter family on the barony of Kilrenny, and his story is soon told. The boat and his companions sank together; but at that very moment it seemed as if a strong hand had thrown deliverance to him out of the darkness, and breasting the waves on some floats which had become wrapped about him, he escaped with his life. A touching visitation was also long remembered by the winter fire. It occurred in the early years of the "sea dearth," when the herring, especially in the spring months, was often as scarce as the haddock. In this dilemma the cod and ling fishers baited their big hooks with the crab or "partane," which was fished by one of the crew in rotation working the creels while the boats were at sea. One day this solitary duty had fallen to the lot of broad-shouldered David Brown. The yawl was almost a stone cast in the offing of the little rock islet known as the Basket, and his neighbour saw him busy first with one trap and then with another, when, like a sudden flash, he tumbled over the gunwale, and disappeared in the sea. It was in full sight of the shore, and boat after boat raced to the scene, but all that could be done was to search for and recover the body. And this was soon accomplished, when the fatal secret was at once explained, for it seems that on returning the " fished" creel to the water the string or messenger had entangled with a button of his sea jacket, and thus in a moment of unsuspected danger, the hapless mariner was dragged into an untimely grave. In after years this occurrence was not the less memorable for a strange fatality, by which the father, as we now see, and his son and grandson all perished within gun-shot of the fatal shore.

CHAPTER VIII,

THE WRECKS AT CELLARDYKE HARBOUR.

We now pass on to notice two of the saddest tragedies that ever occurred on the Fifeshire coast. The scene of both was the old harbour of Cellardyke, where the first occurred on the 23d of September 1793, when seven men perished, and one survived, and the other on a February morning in the year 1800, or less than seven years later, when, by an extraordinary coincidence, seven men were again lost, and only one was saved. The earlier catastrophe, as may be inferred, was towards the close of the Lammas drave, which, as we have seen, has always been the great harvest of the shore. In those years, however, it was as much, if not more so, to the tradesman than with the fishers of the East of Fife; in fact, from Anstruther to Kingsbarns not a loom was in gear, not a lingle in birse, nor an axe and saw at work during the progress of the herring season. And this was not all, for if it so chanced that the weaver had been succeeding with his "customer wark," the souter's wife had nursed the child of a richer neighbour, or the wright had turned the penny in the last bargain with the laird and his trees, then it was the proudest day with the household, as being the first stepping stone to comfort and independence, to transfer the little hoard "from the hugger or the kist neuk" to the purchase of boat and gear.

These herring masters realised in the village or the barony what the poet has so eloquently sung of the yeoman in his shire; but be this as it may, none of the brave old race is so well remembered as the worthy Cellardyke wright, Alexander

Wood, who with six companions suffered on this fatal
occasion. But let us first glance at the life story of ninety
years ago. Alexander Wood, who is the progenitor of the
numerous fishing family of his name in the East of Fife,
was himself sprung, as there is reason to believe, from the
distinguished Leith family, who first settled on the Fife shores
in the person of the famous old Scottish Admiral, Sir Andrew
of Largo. He was cradled in misfortune, but one lucky day
the young wright met General John Scott of Balcomie, who
was so interested in his story that he engaged him as house
carpenter for the castle, when it was ringing with the life and
beauty of his first wife, the brilliant but ill-fated Lady Mary
Hay. Here he woo'd and won winsome Janet Galloway, one
of the domestics from the Carse of Gowrie, with whom he
removed to commence business and housekeeping in Cellardyke.
" He's a usefu' man, Saunders," said the neighbours, as they
saw him one day busy on the cabin of the new sloop, which
Skipper Jack built in the yard above Craignoon, and the next
perhaps hard at work on Stephen Williamson's barn, or again
filling up a spare hour with such kindly offices as came so often
to his hand as mending the spinning wheel or the creepy of
the poor widow, or the lonely one that could only reward him
with her blessing.

" He's a discreet man, Saunders," added the sagacious but
fiery minister, William Beat, while referring to a sederunt of
the Kirk-Session, which he attended after his election as one
of the elders of the parish. Nevertheless he and the old
Presbyter did not always coincide in the same opinion, as the
following curious anecdote will tell :—A lone woman, overwhelmed, as charity is willing to believe, with misery and
isolation, sick and weary, in short, of the great burthen, had
first attempted self-destruction with a knife, and then accom-

plished it by hanging herself from a beam in the old house yet standing in George Street.

At this time the law continued so inexorable that it denied interment in the churchyard to the suicide, whose remains were usually buried in some old march or waste by the sea. Alexander Wood, however, thought and felt like a true Christian, and it is not forgotten that he went three several times to the manse to plead that the remains of the poor woman might be laid to rest amongst her kindred; but the old minister, then verging on eighty, would not consent, and so the corpse, wrapped about and blood besmeared as it was cut down, was dragged through the window, and a hasty grave being scooped out near the golden strand, the body of poor Maggie Lawson was thrown in and covered up with as little ceremony as the carcase of a dog. The companions of such a man as Alexander Wood, whether on sea or shore, were sure to have more or less of his own character or sympathies, and accordingly when circumstances enabled him to launch his stout herring boat the crew was from the first spoken of as amongst the most sedate and cautious on the coast.

But on that bleak September morning they alone had faced the storm. The reason, however, is not far to seek. It was the last chance to save their nets, which were anchored not far from the shore. Still they were seen to hesitate before they began to climb down the rugged pier to gain the boat; but remembering what they had to secure in the way of home comforts they at last pushed to sea. Most of them were landsmen, but the oars were plied so well that they had reached the outside of the skerries. The danger, indeed, was seemingly passed, when a great wave rose, like a ruthless enemy, and with scarce a moment's warning hurled her back upon the beacon rock. A weary cry echoes along the beach, to which the neighbours rush in breathless haste in all directions. "**A** boat, a boat !" shouts an excited voice, and a hundred willing hands spring responsive to the call. But the task is in vain, and brave men stand still in anguish and despair. Here the children, the little children, sob and cling to their mothers, who rend the heavens with the wail of lamentation and woe ; there on the bulwark a paralytic old man kneels and prays in his night clothes, as his grey hairs stream out in the bleak wind ; and yonder on the pier a distracted wife, soon to be a mother, strives to bury her agony in the cruel sea, till she falls fainting in the arms of those around her.

It was the visitation of mercy, and her eye is shut. The foaming waves are swift as the messengers of fate on the path of destruction. And the struggle is short and decisive ; one strong swimmer flings his arms in the air and disappears for ever. Two bosom friends cling together on the broken gun-wale ; but what is devotion and sacrifice to the pitiless surge ? and they die together. A firm foot has gained a rock ; but the enemy is on his trail, and the hapless fisher rolls back a bleeding and bruised corpse ; and so the crew one by one perished, with the solitary exception of the youth James Martin, who is borne up amidst all the death and terror of the storm, as if an angel hand had been outstretched for his deliverance, till he landed unharmed on the high rock to leeward of the harbour.

Amongst those who suffered with Alexander Wood were the Anstruther shoemaker, Thomas Baldie, and Robert Donaldson, weaver, residing in Cellardyke. They, like the skipper and two others of the crew, were married—the household bereavements being in all five widows and seventeen orphan children. The survivor, James Martin, continued to make the sea the calling of his life. He was an honest and deserving man, and

C

marrying in his native town became the father of a family, who lived to do him honour; but his end was so far a tragic one; his grave is with the stranger—having fallen a victim to the dreadful visitation of cholera at the herring rendezvous of Wick in the Lammas of 1832. The second disaster by a singular coincidence has all the sad and thrilling horror of the first. The boat in this case was one of the seven engaged that spring from Cellardyke in the "keeling" or great line fishery. Then as now herring bait was indispensable for the big hooks; but the drift being undreamed of it was fished according to ancient custom by nets anchored perhaps within hail of the shore. The boat was returning that fatal morning from this duty in the face of a rising south-east gale, when, on nearing the harbour, she was overwhelmed by a terrific wave, which swept her from the fairway towards the deadly reef, "the Skellie Point." A death cry is on the sea, and a widow's shriek is on the shore, for who can stay the avalanche? and all is lost—rudderless and disabled the boat is crushed like frost work on the fatal rock. And the neighbours, foreseeing the danger, men and women have clambered on the pier, but no boat can brave that raging sea. "A rope; a net will save them," shouts one; but, alas! it was all in vain. "I see't the noo," said an eye witness hiding her face over the terrible scene of her girlhood, sixty years before, but fresh and vivid as of yesterday. "The cry's in my lug yet," wept another after a still longer interval; and well may they have done so, for there at the feet of wives and children are the perishing ones, calling to them almost by name in their last agony, or with a look more melting still because of the unspoken prayer, as there in the seething waters they sink with all life's jewels, full in sight of home and comfort, into the weary grave. And so the death scene closes on one and all, save the solitary swimmer, William Watson, whose escape is one of the most romantic incidents of the coast. His companions had disappeared in the recoiling waves, but anticipating this danger he bade them all farewell, and divesting himself of his big jacket, plunged into the sea. " I felt as if I walked on the water," he told his friends, and so it almost seemed to others, so strangely was he borne on the great billow that swept him to the shore. Here another thrilling scene occurred. His devoted wife, Mary Galloway, had been one of the spectators of the fatal scene, and now in the heroism of woman's love, and with a strength that was not to be resisted by those around her, she rushed in to his rescue, and clasped him to her bosom, with no thought but the overflowing joy of the moment. Singular as it may appear, he stepped almost on the very spot of the craw skellie on which his townsman, James Martin, had landed as the single survivor seven years before.

William Watson, "Water Willie," as he was usually called after his extraordinary escape, was a fine specimen of a Scottish fisherman, one whose courage and endurance was as conspicuous as his strength and activity. He survived his faithful wife about two years, and died on the second of February 1850, at the good old age of 77.

The sufferers by the calamity of 1800 were—Philip Anderson, Leslie Brown, William Muir, Thomas Fowler, Thomas Smith, Thomas Christie, Andrew Robertson, most of whom being married men no fewer than three-and-thirty orphans were cast on the fatherhood of God.

Here the mournful record is so far complete ; but in the earlier losses tradition has not even preserved the names of many, or rather of most of the victims. Some, however, still linger, like a far away echo, in the old familiar scenes. One of these is Skipper John Tarvit, the father-in-law of the gifted master in the navy, Robert Lothian, whose memory dwells in many a kindly deed on Anstruther shore. Another is John Gardner, who came to Cellardyke to seek a home, but found a grave.   There is also John Moncrieff, the gallant young fisher, who perished before the birth of his son Alexander, who taught the alphabet to three generations, and the art of navigation to more sea heroes than perhaps any other in Scotland.   Aged friends have likewise often told us of the Kilrenny weaver, William Paterson, whose success at the herring fishing season after season was the talk of the coast, but who perished in one of the last days he was to tempt the seas. A yet more melancholy interest, however, is attached to the fate of this old father of the village.   His sons clave to the land, but his grandchildren and great grandchildren of the name, who took to sea, have all perished in the waves.

CHAPTER IX.

THE WAR TIMES, THE PRESS-GANG, AND THE HEROES AND HEROINES OF THE SEA.

And so the end of the century came to us, as we see, in darkness and sorrow. Surely it was as the gathering night to the joyful birth, when the rising hopes were like sunlight on sea and shore, but which one by one had disappeared, before what, in many an eye, were the shadows of despair. Hunger and hardship were already ever widening, ever blackening by the mariner's hearth, where women and children were also weeping for the comfort and joy lost for ever in the storm, or in the battle that was rolling afar. The harbour, the avenue of fisher life, was deserted by all but seven, and not always seven weary crews, the symbol of the shore being but too truthfully the bulwark, and that old man sitting on the broken mast, musing alone on the memories, the fading memories of other and happier years.

But our century is born, "and how shall we welcome the stranger?" We repeat the question as it drops almost at the natal hour from the Parliamenter, Sir John, at the grand supper to his constituents, the Town Council, in the dingy old Tolbooth. It is a great occasion, and he spoke like the friend of Pitt concerning Napoleon, as the evil star that had risen to embroil and desolate Europe, and that his sympathisers at the door, the "Black Nebs," as he contemptuously calls them, were the enemies, not of their country only, but of mankind. He filled in, or rather coloured the picture of the times, and concluded by calling upon his enthusiastic hearers to remember the glorious traditions of their country, and if

need were to draw the sword to uphold and defend the right,
till the God of battles, who was with them, would establish
victory and peace on the downfall and ruin of their enemies.

"Grand speech," hiccuped the landward Bailie on the
Tolbooth stair. " It's easy speakin'," curtly responds a brother
of the sea—the flickering oil lamp at the moment betraying
the bitter look on his honest face.   And no marvel that it was
so, for within the last four-and-twenty hours his brother and
his sister's son had been seized, the one by the press-gang, who
had attacked the house at midnight, and the other by the gun
brig, which lay disguised like a collier in the offing.

He was not alone, however, in his anger and grief; on the
contrary, on that night, and all through the twenty years of
the hot French war, impressment in the King's ships was the
scourge and terror of the coast— the press-gang, in short,
being more feared than the tempest or the raging sea.   Party
politics, it is true, might and did secure the privileged few, as
in the case of the Town Councillor, by certificate or "protection ;" but as a rule the blockade runner was never more
alert and watchful than the fishers of Fife at their lawful
calling against the surprise by the cruizers specially appointed
for the defence of the coast.   The fisher had in the rising
breeze perhaps little to fear, for the smartest frigate or cutter
in the service was no match for his trim little boat, just as on
the bleak autumn day the old commodore, in pity for their
forlorn situation, as he thought, hailed the Cellardyke crew,
" I'll heave to, men, and give you a convoy under close-reefed
topsails to the land."   "Aye, aye, sir," cried little Skipper
Murray, with a quiet laugh, as he and the crew worked the
fishing gear, when, "the last end" on board, the race began.
The old commodore was proud of his corvette, as you could see
by his walk on the quarter deck ; but he turns and stops, when

there, sitting right in the wind's eye, the little craft skims away on the waters like a sea bird on the wing. At his quick order busy hands are on the reef points, and the broad sail springs up the mast. The topgallant sails also curl and fly from the yards till "sheet home" rings far over the sea. The royals also tug at the lofty mast, and yet after all the boat is not to be over-hauled, but sinks into a speck far on the weather bow. "There it comes at last, men," said Skipper Murray, as the wind sweeps down from the west; he is unshipping the rudder at the bulwark, as he says so ; but it was not for another ten days or more that the corvette, caught far to leeward by the gale, was able to cast anchor in the rendezvous at Leith Roads. The tale, how-ever, had another turn in slanting winds or a sudden calm, when an armed pinnace or shotted gun would place an iron hand on the collar of the best and bravest of the crew, who would in this way go out in the morning, but would not return till years of absence on a foreign station, or a French prison as it might chance to be—that is to say, if he returned at all, which many a husband and father, alas ! never did in that long and bloody war.

But the press-gang was more hated than all, for the sailors so employed were usually the most reckless in the ship, who, fired with drink and armed to the teeth, would steal into the town at midnight, and attack the houses like the onslaught of robbers or pirates. They were also in league with secret spies, who chalked the door of an intended victim. Is resist-ance possible ? It is not ; and the unfortunate mariner is dragged away by the drunken ruffians, who have struck down the poor wife and the children, clinging to him in their anguish and despair. At times, however, a different reception is in wait for them. A friendly scout has advertised the coming, and the inhabitants, true to the heroic old days, when the

Laird of Wemyss and the fishers of Fife routed the English,
as one to five on the brae above St Monance kirk, rose to the
danger, and more than once the officer and his crew have
been seen flying through the gullet at the old East Green
with showers of stones pelting at their heels, the ready
artillery of the wives of Cellardyke, with gown tails well filled
from the sea beach ; or, again, it has been the fishers and
their boat hooks bearing down all before them, like the
Scottish spearsmen in the wars of "Wallace wight." Stratagem
is also tried, and in the necessities of their situation every
house, as in the smuggling days with its "gin or brandy hide,"
has now its secret recess or trap-door, now cunningly contrived
under the bed clothes ; now under that big chest in the dark
corner, by which, like the subterranean passage of a besieged
castle, the hardy fisher could at a moment's notice retreat
from the enemy.

Conflicts like these are more harassing than the winter
storm, because they have to be wedged, not now and then,
but in all times and seasons. Yet after all there is another
and a more indiscriminate enemy sitting like the wolf at the
open door. Here is a suggestive anecdote to illustrate our
meaning :—A few years later a Cellardyke boat is weathering
the then desolate Inchcape reef, when one of the crew com-
plained of the long and hazardous sea, and the little recom-
pense that came by it. " Don't grumble, David," said the old
skipper—" don't grumble, your father and I have parted
coppers many a day."

They had brave Scottish hearts, however, these old fisher
folk, and knew how to meet and conquer in the battle.

There was an orphan household with three sisters, " as
bonnie strappin' lasses as in Cellardyke," said our dear old
friend, but with a single Sunday gown amongst them. In

this dilemma the prized garment was worn by the sister whose turn and privilege it was every third Sabbath to go to the church; but they were contented rather to have it so than be indebted to any one, and thus to wait and suffer, sustained by the hope, which did not fail, " God," they said, will help us to kindlier days.

Here is another peep into the inner life of the heroic past : —In order to sweeten the long and irksome hours in the days of the hand-wrought net, the young women of Cellardyke would assemble in a neighbour's to ply the busy needle. A favourite trysting-place was a house near the Urquhart Wynd, inhabited by a widow and her two daughters, who earned their livelihood by what to their companions was little else than the occupation of an idle hour. The little party, of course, broke up at meal time, when the others went home to the comforts of the tea table, but with the widow's household there was only the solace of a dry crust and water as it came from the spring; yet rather than that any human eye should see or suspect the sacrifice which they made for an honest upholding, a wet cup was taken to daub and sprinkle the table as if they also had enjoyed their own full share of the dainties of life.

But here we have the secret of the strengthened courage of the sea-side homes of Fife.

The aged mother of one of the sufferers towards the close of the century was left with the snows of eighty on her venerable head without a friend or stay in this world. She inhabited a cold and cheerless apartment, in which even, in the dead of winter, she could scarcely find fuel for a fire. Still, she was content to suffer rather than to beg or let her wants be known; but one day the parish minister, James Forrester, called to see her. He looked around him, the north wind was keen and sharp, but the hearth was cold and desolate. " Have you nothing left of comfort ? " said the minister, touched to the heart with pity. " Oh, aye, sir, there's the back-door and the promises," answered the old saint, her eyes brimming and beaming with tears, as she referred to the sanctuary where she so often knelt and prayed in the abiding peace and joy in " Our Father which art in Heaven."

A period of fully five years elasped after the disaster of 1800 before another catastrophe darkened the homes of Cellardyke. At the time the big boats were reserved for the drave, or perhaps the " kellin lines," while the haddock fishery was plied by a class of swift but trusty yawls like the St Monance fishers of later years. It was on the 24th of June 1805 that one of the nine boats so employed from Cellardyke was seen and recognised from the famous outlook, the Castle-yard of Crail. She was the " Nancy," owned by the brothers, Alexander & Thomas Scott, and was in full sail for home, when it disappeared like a snow-flake on the face of the waters. We were once in the same deadly peril. Worn out by the toils of the morning, and seduced by the heat of the day, we had fallen into a kind of waking slumber, which had also overpowered our helmsman, when we were suddenly aroused by the strange wild voices of wind and waters. The black squall was upon us, and each one asleep and careless at his post ; and now, high on the weather side, we look down on the lee wale buried in the green sea, in which pale faces were upturned to Heaven, but so sadly, so sorrowfully, as if they only thought of home and children, naked and desolate for ever. We escaped, but on that fatal day not one was left to tell how six brave men met their fate. The death record is —Alexander Scott, who left a widow and four children ; Thomas Scott, who had a wife and two daughters ; James

Morris, who left a widow and six children, cast on the mercy of Providence ; and three young unmarried men, named David Rhynd, David Wilson, and James Watson.

They lie buried in the deep, except Alexander Scott, whose corpse was seen at sea a few days after the accident, but only recovered five weeks later by the Earl of Kellie's fisher at Fifeness, when it was laid with kindred dust hard by the ancient Lykegate of Kilrenny.

The next casualty, if less disastrous, was akin to the former. It occurred on a harvest morning in the offing of Caiplie ; but all escaped except a gallant youth, named Leslie Brown, whose father and grandfather, as we have seen, also shared a watery grave.

An extraordinary incident here claims a place in our narrative. When overset by the squall the boat, which was named the "Brothers" of Cellardyke, rapidly filled and sank ; but in the all-terrible excitement of the moment Robert Anderson had the singular presence of mind to unclasp the knife and cut the lines which entangled him to the wreck. He returned the knife half shut to its place in his jacket, which he next threw off to swim for his life ; but so vividly had his every act been stamped upon his memory that the knife was found in the pocket as he said when the jacket was raised with the boat in the course of the following week.

Our mournful chronicle and the interval has nothing on which to dwell, but carries us down to the closing day of the eventful year 1814. The occasion is the Burntisland herring fishery, or the famous "up the water drave ;" but before proceeding with the narrative let us briefly refer to an enterprise so much entwined with the fisher life of the Fife coast. The fishery began in 1793, but twenty years before the sea so swarmed with herrings that, according to the story, an old sailor once dipped his mainsail into Inverkeithing bay to wash away the coal dust, and to his surprise and delight caught them in dozens in the folds of the canvass. The East Neuk laughed at the yarn; but the cunning fisher of Donibristle, Tam Brown, knew and kept the secret; he even cast aside hook and line to dip and fish the herring with a pail, till his neighbours at last set watch and detected his selfish trick, which, coming to the ears of the starving fishers of Queensferry, led to the first trial at the time in question with the net. The discovery thus made flew, as good news always fly, along the coast, and so, while some were incredulous in Cellardyke, "too good news to be true," they said, others hastened to the Braehead to fasten rope and yarn, and then hied away, with the same ardour as their grandchildren in recent years, to the gold fields of Australia. The herrings were in boatloads, but the price was often only half-a-crown a barrel; but next winter and next such fleets of Greenock smacks and Irish wherries came through the canal that the market rose to half-a-guinea, and in later years to more than a guinea a cran. It was new life to the shore, as it enabled the household to rise above the calamity of a luckless Lammas drave, or it might be to retrieve the misfortunes of the last Greenland voyage; and if all did not, and do not, draw prizes in the sea lottery, still in some cases, at least, the "up the water drave" proved the "nest egg" of after prosperity and riches. In 1814, to which our narrative refers, the chances of the sea had been rather discouraging; but the Elie packet had brought down good news on the Saturday, and accordingly every crew that could muster was up and away on Monday morning. It was a strong wind from the westward, but boat after boat was gallantly weathering the stream, when about a mile to leeward of Inchkeith one of them was caught and upset by a sudden squall.

The ferry boat was at once to the rescue, and a strong swimmer is saved, but his young companion sinks as the friendly rope falls on his shoulder. A death grasp is on some floating wreck, and the corpse of the skipper was recovered. This was David Roger, who, with his noble boy George, and a fine young man named Thomas Watson, are the victims of this fatal voyage.

The only survivor is Thomas Smith, whose life story has an interest and pathos all its own. While a lad of fifteen he had stood on Cellardyke pier and heard the death cry and seen the last wrestle of his poor father in the awful tragedy of 1800. He himself had been a castaway in the midnight wreck of the Leith smack near Stonehaven, when all on board had perished on the stormy lee, and when he had also been taken for a bruised corpse by the lady that chance, or rather Providence, had sent, she knew not why, that morning to the lonely shore. This remarkable man was spared to the patriarchial age of four score and four—his death taking place on the 19th of March 1869.

The boat, which had been built but a short time before by Bailie Paton, of Anstruther, was recovered, but was subsequently lost with all hands while fishing years after from Pittenweem. David Rodger left an orphan household of five sons and three daughters; but his widow, Elizabeth Watson, was one of those heroines who rise to struggle when others would sink in despair. She wept away the tears in the sweet and abiding promise of Him who says, " I am with thee," and so wrought and sacrificed, but surely not in vain, even on this side of the river. David, at nineteen, became from that day the breadwinner of the family, while his four younger brothers —Alexander, James, Thomas, and Robert—took in time to shipboard, and before she died the widow had the pride and pleasure of seeing one and all in command of foreign-going ships.

Had this misfortune occurred a year earlier, the fishing fleet of Cellardyke would not have numbered so many as Sir Robert Sibbald saw it a hundred years before ; but at this time many an old face had returned to the bulwarks that had been a stranger for many a year.   These were the sailors who had been so ruthlessly dragged away by the press-gang, but who, nevertheless, had done their duty with the bravest, whether in the battle or the storm ; who had seen Nelson's glorious watchword, and sent back an answering cheer in the thunder of Trafalgar; or who had also fought and bled in the thousand conflicts which had made the " meteor flag " the terror and glory of the seas.

It was a proud privilege to be a listener by the old pier in these days.   Here is one, for instance, telling an ancient crony of his last year's herring cruise at Wick, perhaps as one of the five hands of Thomas Cunningham's drave boat, the "Jennet," a staunch and serviceable craft, though scarcely eight-and-twenty feet of keel.   " What gear did ye carry ?" asks the friend. " Oh, three nets to a man—one fifty yards and the other two forty yards long, but all fifteen score deep ;" and then, perchance, would follow the usual bitter complaint about the dearth of the times, which had raised the pound of hemp to the ransom price of a shilling—the spinning of the same to sixpence and the laying to threepence.   " Oor folk wroucht my new net," the speaker would continue, but he would tell his friend that the ordinary rate when others had to be employed was sixpence the yard or the half pound of hemp— that is to say, when the worker was to be paid by weight instead of by the measure.   The conversation would then likely con- clude with a reference to the success of the drave, in which some boats had fished and others had not fished their complement of two hundred barrels—the price having advanced that year from eight shillings to ten shillings a barrel. At another corner, perchance, the talk is about the increasing size of the boats, and the last addition is emphatically pointed to on the beach. She is the leviathan of the coast at a length of twenty-nine feet, but old David Birrel, who is accepted as one of the best authorities in Cellardyke, has given his unreserved opinion after walking round and round the new craft, " She's too big, I say, either to row or sail."

Here some passing incident has thrown the " crack " into another channel, and reference is next made to the forlorn state of the cooper trade. Now that the herrings had forsaken the old haunts of Fife, and perhaps to an inquiry after Robert Tod or John Darsie, the reply would be that like his neighbours he had taken to a West India or Greenland voyage, seeing that, like Othello, " his occupation was gone." In all probability one of the group would tell us something very singular, that he could recollect when Bailie William Russell had cured two hundred barrels, as he did on the Lammas of 1802, at the Brae of Anstruther. But the group is never so large or so closely drawn under the lea of the " craw skellie," nor is the interest so deep and all absorbing, as when the returned warriors fight their battles o'er again. And little marvel it is so remembering what they have to tell of flood and field. Here, for instance, is the life sketch of one. It is dark-haired David Wilson, who has come on the errand of love to Cellardyke. This hero was born in the ever-memorable year 1792 at Brownhills, by the glorious sea shore of St Andrews. His father, a fine specimen of the Scottish cottar, was foreman on the farm ; but the " hairst rig " or the green knowes, had no charms for the dark-haired

herd-boy as compared with the flashing main, with the ships
coming and going like " things of life and light ; " and so one
evening, when only twelve years of age, he left his father's
roof-tree to begin life as a sailor.   His first floating home was
the little bluff Kirkcaldy smack, the " Maggie Lauder,"
which in these days was thought big enough to charter to
London ; but though no drudge or dog is kicked about like
the cabin boy of a coaster, David stuck with a hero's heart
to his first love till by a lucky chance he improved his situation on board an over sea trading brig belonging to Dunbar.
While voyaging in his craft he was one stormy day thrown
from the top-gallant yard into the sea, where he manfully
buffeted for a weary hour and a quarter with the hungry
billows before he could be rescued, more dead than alive ; but
notwithstanding all such stern experience and still more his
mother's melting tears, the young rover remained true to old
Neptune, and on the first opportunity extended his voyages
by joining the gallant old " Advice " of Dundee in a whaling
cruise to Greenland.   These were the stirring days of the
French war and the press-gang, when the British sailors had
often as much reason to fear a friend as a foe, and so it happened one September day with the crew of the old Tay
whaler, who, instead of the wistfully watched-for hills of Scotland, saw the dreaded war brig " Pickle " lurking like a wolf in
their track.   David Wilson and his comrades did not need to
be told her errand, and, as the only hope of escape, the old
ship was instantly trimmed under all sail right before the
freshening breeze.   As quickly up flew top-gallant and stud-
ding sail on the brig, which followed in the chase like a
hound at the heels of a wild boar, as the rising gale swelled
the broad mainsail of the old hulk till tack and sheet
snapped again, and her huge sides were fairly buried in

foam and spray, and yet after all her fleet pursuer proudly
ranged alongside. " Round to," thundered the captain
through his speaking trumpet from the quarterdeck ; but
David, who was at the helm, only grasped the wheel with a
firmer hold, and, with " no surrender" stamped on every
feature of his manly face, kept the ship steady on her course,
while the seamen, handspike in hand, by way of *ruse*, drove
the honest-hearted St Monance master and the other officers
into the cabin, to save them from the serious consequence of
disobeying orders from a king's ship. Being thus defied, the
brig was next steered across the bows of the whaler, as if to bar
her further flight, but on swept the whaleship like a maddened
bull, straight to the assault, and the cruiser's helm was put
down just in time to avert the collision. " Round to, or I'll
sink you," again thundered from the quarterdeck ; but even
the ship boy, fired with the wild enthusiasm of the moment,
waved defiance from the yard-arm. The insulted Captain was
furious with rage, and the shotted guns were opened upon the
fugitive ship. "Whizz, whizz," flew the deadly shower, but the
courageous steersman never flinched from his post. Though one
bullet and then another struck the spoke from his hand, he as
quickly seized another, and kept the gallant old craft bounding
before the blast till sail and rigging was riddled by cannon shot,
and the disabled hulk lay at the mercy of the war brig, who completed the capture at the point of the cutlass. The intrepid
steersman was, of course, regarded as the head mutineer, and
as such was treated, or rather ill-used, by the commander,
who appears to have been quite unworthy of the uniform of
Nelson or Collingwood. He was ordered under irons till he
and his comrades could be tried for mutiny on the high seas,
for so the *ruse* on Captain Adamson of the " Advice" was
held to be, and with this terrible purpose the brig was now

D

steered for the Thames. David also incurred the unbridled vengeance of the Captain by refusing to answer certain questions which would have established the serious crime with which he was charged, and the poor sailor lay day and night with a six-feet iron bar across his legs, and his hands rivetted to the ring bolts, but in this woeful plight he one day found a true and unexpected friend. This was one of the brig's crew who sheltered his fallen head as a London lawyer in the King's service, and who had just been punished for some misconduct by the Captain, towards whom, in consequence, he cherished the bitterest hate. By the counsel of this new friend, the simple young mariner pled so well before the court in London, that he was held to be innocent of mutiny, but at the same time he was forced to enter the King's service on board the "Pickle," though he had the satisfaction to see his enemy, the Captain, cashiered for cruelty and a course of conduct unworthy a British officer. On board the war-brig David was so distinguished as a brave and expert sailor that he was in a fair way of obtaining promotion through the high opinion of his officers, when he and his boat's company resolved to desert the ship, which he accordingly did one night at Jersey, where he also joined a packet holding a letter of marque and trading to the Mediterranean. While crossing the Bay of Biscay the vessel was captured by two French privateers, who soon after put into port with their English prisoners. The unfortunate sailors were driven like a herd of cattle into an ancient church, where, on a scanty truss of straw, they lay down for the night; but some revengeful hand fired the litter, when the old sanctuary was speedily wrapped in flames. David lived to tell the scene which followed, when, as William Tennant sings,

"Pinnacle cam' doon and tow'r,
And Virgin Maries in a shower
Fell flat and smashed their faces."

From this burning pile the prisoners were marched by their vindictive guards to an inland citadel, where they experienced all the horrors of French captivity, till one day the thunder of the British cannon in Wellington's glorious march to Paris opened the doors of their dungeon to the weary captives. At the peace he returned home to his mother, who had taken up house in Pittenweem, where the true-hearted Scottish widow, like many a brave sister in adversity, earned an honest crust by spinning yarn for herring nets. Every Scottish whaler knew the story of David Wilson's dauntless stand at the helm of the " Advice ;" but he was gratified to hear that his Dundee friends had sent his jacket, having in one pocket a bullet extracted from the wheel, and in another a yet weightier gift to his poor parents in Fife ; but for a time his unceremonious leave-taking of the King's service made the East Neuk little else than a hiding place. Eventually, however, his Cellardyke bride induced him to settle there, and to take to life as a fisherman. He was spared to see his children's children grow up to man and woman's estate, and " fell asleep," as softly as he had ever done on his mother's bosom, on the fourth of April 1875, aged eighty-three.

Let us now turn to the tale that is told to us of one of Cellardyke's own gallant sons, Robert Pratt, who, at the age of eleven, left the dingy " ben end," which served as the Parish School of Kilrenny, to begin life as a cabin boy in the Excise yacht " Prince of Wales," the same that is carved on the tombstone of her old commander, David Henderson, in the gable of East Anstruther Church. This was in 1800, when smugglers were almost nightly on the coast, running their cargoes amongst the rocks skirting St Andrews ; but however alert, and often on the track, the old brig was but a lame dog in the chase, and so at the end of four years he quitted the thankless

service for a berth on board of the Dundee whaler, "Mary Ann,"
from which, however, at the end of a single voyage, he was
scared by the press gang, who at this time kept a cat-like
watch on the Greenland ships.   He took refuge, as it were, in
the forecastle of the Leith and London trader, the "Hope," but
before weathering Inchkeith the young smacksman was seized
by a lieutenant and his crew of the old "Ardent," which was
then lying as a guardship in Leith Roads.   Robert, as one of
the smartest lads of the ship, was called to duty as a petty
officer ; but impressment was to him, as to every brave spirit,
the iron yoke of bondage, to which he could never be reconciled.
Love, all-conquering love, was also in the struggle ; in fact,
he had just espoused a winsome damsel of St Andrews, and
being thus ready to dare and do to the uttermost for his
liberty he actually leaped from the fore chains of the guardship on to the rigging of the ferry smack, which had tacked
at the instant under her lee.   The friendly gale soon landed
him at Kinghorn, when, in the full realisation of his peril, he
hastened away to the muirs of Fife, where, like a criminal
escaping for his life, he took the most unfrequented paths, till
the early hours of Sabbath morning saw him once more safe
across his father's threshold in Cellardyke.   By the con-
nivance of his St Andrews friends he obtained a berth in a
coasting schooner bound to London ; but the Thames had
been scarcely reached when he was once more impressed for
the royal service, the ship being the "Thetis."   He had seen a
younger brother dragged like a felon up the gangway three
days after his own seizure in the "Ardent ;" and now his
captivity, as he felt it, was shared by his old school companion, Thomas Watson, but both being of the same sanguine
and resolute character, an escape was at once resolved upon, and
so within a fortnight the first dark night found them with

their clothes bag in their teeth stealing through the hawse-hole, where the cable gave them a ready access to the stream. The frigate was lying about half-a-league from Greenwich, and there in the darkness and the rushing tide-way the swim for life begins. One leads, and the other as bravely follows; but a death cry is on the wave, "Oh, Lord God, have mercy upon me," and with the words upon his lips poor Tom sinks into a watery grave. Weary and sad Robert gained the bank, where, as he wiped away the tear for his unfortunate companion, he was accosted by a party of chimney sweeps travelling to London. Pity is a jewel of heaven's own setting in the humblest bosom, and so these waifs of the city stopped to light a fire to dry the clothes and give a warm drink to the poor fugitive. He had little difficulty in finding a situation on board one of the Greenwich whalers, from which he next removed his sea chest to a grand old troopship, which became his floating home for the next five years. One unlucky day, however, he was induced to enter as the mate of a collier brig, which on his first voyage was run into and carried during the night by a French privateer, swarming with men, seen, indeed, the day before, but jested over as the most unsailor like ship of the convoy. The prisoners were landed in France, but only to be hurried within the hour on a three hundred miles march into the interior. It was the dead of winter, and badly lodged and worse fed the poor sailors were so exhausted that, unable to walk, they staggered along, struck and kicked at like over-driven cattle by their mounted guard. Their destination was an old fortress; their lodgings a dreary stone-paved chamber at the top of the wall, which they were at first disposed to welcome as "rest at any price" for the sake of their blistered and bleeding feet; but cold and hunger soon made their situation insupportable.

"Better die like men breaking free than starve to death like rats in a hole," exclaimed one of the eighteen captives, and the thought kindling every heart with a blaze of enthusiasm, a scheme was resolved upon that very evening to secure their liberty. A marlin spike, which next to his knife is the sailor's best treasure, had been secreted from their jailors, and by it the iron stanchions which barred the window or rather aperture, which admitted both the blast and the light, was one night loosened and the next removed, when their blankets tied together enabled them to reach the ground. The English sailors almost ruined the exploit by a characteristic cheer, but a raging snow storm befriended the fugitives, and hand in hand they rushed into the darkness. That snow storm was the severest ever known in the country, but night by night they saw in it the hand of Providence. They dug trenches in the drift, in which they lay at once concealed and warm ; but their great difficulty was a supply of food. France was at that hour in the last crisis of her military glory; but greater than the decrees of Napoleon were the decrees of heaven, for the poor French villagers, instead of betraying, helped the poor exiles on their homeward way. As if remembering their own husbands and children in a foreign prison, these women would often assist the sailors from their little stores—their bounty being at times moistened with their tears; but occasionally they had an opportunity of bartering such articles as they had for necessaries of life—their mother-of-pearl buttons being especially valued in the exchange—and so after six weeks of constant suffering and peril they at last gained the coast, when, to their signal joy, they descried an English ship in the offing, and a fisher boat being at hand they were soon safe on board, and within the week were landed at Falmouth.

Robert Pratt returned to Cellardyke, and settled with his family. He took to the whale fishing, and made no fewer than 37 voyages, till he was eventually disabled by an accident. This old sailor is a striking instance of the value of a handicraft to one of his vacation. His sagacious father impressed with this necessity had taught all his sons the art of the sail-maker, which Robert carried on with singular success for many a year. None in particular knew better how to fashion a lug sail, and after being long a household name in the sea homes of Fife, his eventful life closed on the 24th of June 1870, in his eighty-second year.

These veterans were, of course, the heroes of the hour, but nevertheless the fishers of the coast could be more than listeners in the tale of daring and romance.

It is true that no flag of defiance had waved upon the shore. The French war, being thus unlike the former struggle, when, in the autumn of 1779, Paul Jones and his squadron, flying the stars and stripes, rounded to in the offing of Cellardyke, hailed first one boat and then another to send "a pilot on board." The signals, however, were prudently unheeded. "We didn't like the cut of his jib," they said, "but still less the hang-dog faces on the weather gangway;" and the fishermen thus escaped the lure which entrapped the Pittenweem pilot, Jack Paton; or, again, two years later, when the noted privateer, Captain Fall, fired a random shot or two at Anstruther Custom House, which can be traced to this day on the rafters of the grim old tenement at the harbour head. But if Napoleon and his flotilla never came, the inhabitants, like their neighbours, were at least resolved and ready to resist him. At Anstruther and also at Crail there was a volunteer company a hundred strong, and, not behind the landsmen, the fishers of Cellardyke had, in the patriotic ardour of the hour, enrolled into a kind of naval reserve, which had been organised for the defence of the coast. They were carefully instructed by Captain Malone in the use of the boarding pike and the big gun—sometimes in the "fish yard," sometimes at the Billowness—the war spirit being so thoroughly roused in the hearts of young and old that every schoolboy was also a volunteer, marching out and in with the detachment, armed with a long stick, by way of boarding pike, cut that morning, perhaps, from the woods of Innergellie, in utter defiance of the old Laird and all his henchmen. It was not all muster and parade, however ; an order came—an order which was at once and cheerfully obeyed—to embark with the squadron that was sent out to Copenhagen to seize the Danish fleet in 1807. The Cellardyke men won the heart of old Admiral Gambier by the expertness and fidelity which signalised their service and which led to their being appointed in many cases as petty officers on board of prize ships. They especially distinguished themselves in the sharp action with the gallant Danes, but still more in the terrific storm which was encountered on the voyage to England. In fact, under heaven, the safety of several line of battleships and others of the squadron was owing to the presence of mind, and no less conspicuous seamanship, of old Alexander Pratt, the father of our hero, Robert. The three decker was running under close reefed topsails, when Alexander, who was on duty on the foretop, saw in a momentary rift in the darkness the white breakers close on the lee. "Wear the ship ; she's ashore on the Goodwin," he shouted. The steersman hesitates, but an intrepid hand is on the stay, and, springing like a squirrel along the deck, Cellardyke seizes the wheel. "Take care, my lad," said the officer of the watch, drawing a pistol from his breast, but the manœuvre saved the ship and the lives of all on board—nay, the signals now made sent the whole fleet on another tack, and the fatal sandbank was weathered by one and all. Several of the fishers were likewise on board the "Eighty-Four," under the command of the Anstruther hero—Lieutenant, afterwards Sir James, Black—which was caught by the tempest while at anchor in Yarmouth Roads. The best bower was out, but the battleship was fast driving on the sands, and hope with the last gleam of day had forsaken the weary crew. "God help us; we shall never see the morning light again," said the next in command in a husky voice, and the fate of eight hundred men —captors and captives—seemed to be sealed, when James Black snatched an axe, and calling for volunteers, in which he was as bravely answered by his old companions at the "Big Dub," cut away the masts, when, like a forest king stripped off his branches, the ship with her living freight outbraved the storm.

CHAPTER X.

SOWING THE HARVEST—INTERESTING ANECDOTES.

The return of peace was the return of prosperity, and the winter after Waterloo saw more activity at the bulwark and elsewhere on the shores of Fife than had been the case for thirty years before. New and larger boats floated in the harbour, fresh and more seaward fishing fields were explored, not everyday, it is true, with success, as when that trusty old plank, " the Father and Son," was running home from beyond the Bell Rock. " We'd been better at the Glack," said Geordie Anderson, with an eye at the scanty luck. " Haud yer tongue, man," retorted his skipper, Sandy Wood, " it was better times before you or the Glack was heard of ;" the sea referred to being Dunse Law, bearing over the famous ravine at the " Pease Brig," some four leagues to the eastward of the May, which, within his own time, the skipper had regarded almost in the light of a foreign adventure. On the whole, however, hook and line met with fair returns—the harvest of the sea being in those years in happy contrast with the harvest of the land, which was more than once gathered in the East Neuk ankle deep in snow. The whale ship, it is true, yet divided the affections of the coast, so much so that when the first steamboat—the lumbering old tug—rounded the Carr, the people everywhere running out to see the ship on fire, over seventy of our whalers were on board, and these only the contingent from Aberdeen, who had made a bargain on that pier to be landed at Anstruther, which was accordingly done, to the intense delight of the old port. A good Greenland voyage, shall we whisper, was that day the joy of the shore. "It just turned oor hand," said the honest goodwife, in all ages the Chancellor of the Exchequer in the fisher home, and many a time and oft it replenished the "ways and means" for the new fishing tackle, if not for the last year's rent. But we turn to another point. "We could catch fish, but we could not sell them," observes an old friend, referring to the market of his early days. But about this time the curious merchandise known as "couping," that is the system of selling or sending fish from boat to boat, was engaged in with considerable spirit and enterprise on the shores of the Forth. To some extent it was already a century old, for in the event of a good haul and a fair breeze, especially in the summer months, the Cellardyke boats, instead of steering home, would make their landfall at Fisherrow sands, where the North Sea fish, as the Buckhaven and other inshore fishers knew to their loss, as the old minister of Wemyss tells, had the mastery of the Edinburgh market, and not only so, but the celebrated Dr Carlyle of Inveresk is our authority that the Fisherrow boats would sail to the East of Fife, where it was more profitable to buy than to gather the spoils of the deep. The chance run, however, had been superseded by a regular weekly or bi-weekly service, while faithful old William Anderson, from the beach of Queensferry, opened the markets of Glasgow, for which he has had again and again as many as three cargoes afloat in the course of a week. The Dundee and St Andrews cadgers were also at the pier, but the "couper" was the great merchant of the coast, and that from year to year, till the memorable day that the thoughtful Anstruther grocer—Robert Taylor—introduced a new era into the sea industry of the East of Fife. It is a romantic story. Mr Taylor was a passenger in the Leith packet "Maggie Lauder," but Skipper Baynes, after the mooring ropes had been actually

cast loose, resolved, in the change of wind, not to sail till
another day.   In these circumstances, remembering an old
Edinburgh friend, Mr Taylor walked from Leith pier to the
High Street.   He was standing at the friend's counter, when
the guard of the Aberdeen mail coach entered with a parcel
of " Finan haddies," which were evidently as welcome as the
first choice fruits of the season, and the grocer as frankly
yielded to an advance, because, as the guard said, " Haddies
are dear now-a-days at Finan."   " If haddocks are dear at
Finan it is otherwise in Cellardyke," thought Mr Taylor, who
was told by his friend that the guard bought the parcels from
a fisher relative of his wife, and that the little speculation
was to the profit of both.   Then and there it flashed on Mr
Taylor's mind, " Why not send smoked fish from Fife," and,
full of the idea, he returned to Anstruther to try the experiment, first in hogsheads at his own back door, and then in the
premises leased and specially erected at the Brae.   It was a
seedling wafted on the wind, but which in fifty years had so
developed that in a single day—on the 9th of January 1869—
the deep-sea going boats of Cellardyke, then forty-one in number,
landed at Anstruther shore over fifty tons of " caller haddies "
—the prime take being thirty-nine hundredweight, which sold
at the ruling price of 10s a hundredweight, or £500 in all—the
enormous catch, almost to a tail, passing into the hands of
one or other of the local curers, in order to be consigned as
" smeekit haddies," the great change since Mr Taylor's day
being that Glasgow had taken the place of Auld Reekie.
Robert Taylor was associated in this enterprize with
another who also claims a word of kindly remembrance.
This is Captain Robertson, who, as an apprentice lad noted
for his spirit and energy, had cast in his lot for life with a
Norlan lass in Edinburgh, but an encounter one evening in

the High Street changed the current of his destiny. He awoke next morning with the badge of the East India Company on his bonnet, and within a week had embarked for Madras. Repentance came, as repentance often comes, when too late, and he gave himself up to sadness and despair. The ship was boarded and taken by the enemy, but he refused to stir a finger, and kept his berth. A little Frenchman dealt the broken spirited soldier a contemptuous blow on the head with a hatchet. It was his last blow, for, springing up like a roused lion, Captain Robertson killed him on the spot with his own hatchet, and, almost single handed, saved the ship. Promotion followed, and after a distinguished career in India he once more sailed for the old country. Poor Maggie Sutherland, at this time neither wife nor widow, had from first to last a weary life ; but she had one happy day when, as the house drudge, she came to open the door for the gallant officer who called in the carriage—that officer being her own husband, and his errand to bring her home. He had retired from active service, but a curious chain of circumstances induced him to turn his thoughts to sea merchandise at Anstruther. " I like the place and I like the people," and throwing his whole soul into the enterprise, he soon gave a new cast to the fortunes of the shore. He was the first to break the close league among the coupers, and nothing fired his indignation so much as an attempt to overreach the fishermen, when his ringing voice would give a new turn to the prices of the day. His stature was prodigious. " A bottle of brandy, Captain, that you outweigh the giant boy," exclaimed his waggish friend, David Rodger, when the town's folks had turned out to see and wonder at the public exhibition. The good humoured veteran submitted to the test in full sight of the crowd, when he was seen to have the advantage of three stones, or thirty-three to thirty over the famous English giant.   He had a heart, however, as soft and tender as a child, and none save the eye of heaven knew how truthfully he was one of the noble few that

"Do good by stealth and blush to find it fame;"

but, to the grief of all, he, one fatal morning in the Lammas of 1823, soon after the death of his friend Robert Taylor, leaped in delirium over the old pier at Anstruther, when his troubled spirit passed to the mercy seat of God.

It was an anecdote of the bookseller's shop at Anstruther shore that the "Finan haddie" was so highly esteemed by the reigning sovereign—George the Fourth—that the mail-coach as regularly as the letter-bag, carried a prime parcel from the little Banchory village for the royal breakfast.   The waggish collector told a stupid joke that "Letter Maggie" had been seen freighted from the post-office with a mysterious packet, which was nothing less than a royal order to have the palace supplied from Anstruther; but although it had been really so, the Captain could never have been more enthusiastic about his fish-house and kiln, which is, after all, the secret of the early and exultant success of the Anstruther experiment.

Originally, however, Captain Robertson's eye, like that of the other merchants of the coast, had been all upon the cod fishery, which was so extensive that the prince of Scottish fishcurers, James Methuen, had christened Cellardyke "the cod emporium of Scotland."   That fishery had long been the backbone of the coast; but new energy had been infused into it by the establishment of the Fishery Board in 1808, or rather by the amendment of the Act in 1815, which struck off the iron shackles, so long and firmly rivetted by the old law, framed in the worst spirit of the times. As examples in point, it strictly prohibited the English rock salt, so indispensable to-day; it left the fishcurer no choice but to use "the fushionless saut wi' nae deed," as the old coopers would say, manufactured at Pittenweem, or the other salt pans of the coast, and at the same time it burthened the trade with a tax on the first and last necessity of the cure. Under the new system, however, thousands of barrels with the cod in pickle were freighted every Lent to London, the Fife cure being noted far and near for its sweetness and perfection. These were, in truth, rising days for the coast, as the Lammas drave also began to revive about this time. Wick was still the favourite rendezvous; but a little squadron fished the returning shoals from Cellardyke with encouraging luck, while under the new Fishery Act the merchant had as many, nay more, encouragements to speculate than he had in the cod and ling fishery, the salt tax, in particular, being before so oppressive that it actually took a shilling out of the blistered hand of the poor cottar every time his "gudewife" filled the herring barrel. Herrings were freely cured for the brand, and smoking houses also began to be erected on the coast. Inspector Loch in 1778, as we saw, talks of such a purpose; but it was full twenty years later till the first kiln was erected in the rear of the old custom-house on Anstruther shore. It was built for the "John aboon the braes," in the curious old rhyme concerning the Robertsons of Anstruther :—

"Here's Paul John, and Pamf John, and John aboon the braes,
And John Robertson, the dyster, that dyes thread to sew our claes."

The artisan was a Dunbar sailor, named James Swanson, who, while sitting during an after hour on the "Skipper's Rest" at the old gable, was fond of telling the curious story, according to which the merchants of Yarmouth, in the days of King Charles, had sent to Dunbar for tutors in the art of making bloaters; but the shoals deserted the coast season after season,

till the work and the workers were forgotten, so much so that
when the herrings came again to the Forth, Dunbar had
actually to send to Yarmouth to borrow back the secret from
the descendants of her own children, who in the interval had
made Yarmouth bloaters famous the wide world over. The
fishery and the kiln failed together, but within the
next twenty years Mr Robertson's son-in-law, Bailie John
Darsie, resumed the speculation in the old man's garden,
which in this particular may be regarded as the nest of the
fishcuring enterprise of our day. As usual the return of the
herring was the return of life and energy to the shore. The
successful drave of 1816 inspired the laurel crown in the
celebrated Musiemanik Society of Anstruther. The poet sings—

> " What time the Fifian plains, with plenty crowned,
>   Change their green aspect for a yellower hue,
>   The hardy weather-beaten fisherman,
>   Tired of the haddock and the petley tribe,
>   And red-ware codling from the town of Crail,
>   Or rocky Cellardyke, walks anxious forth,
>   And from the windmill or the castle yard
>   Peers o'er the ocean, hopeful to espy
>   Some well-known symptom of the herring race ;
>   Nor looks he long in vain ; the enormous whale
>   Spouts briny fountains from his nostril wide ;
>   Wheel-like the awkward porpoise by the shoal
>   Of countless millions rolls ; the cunning seal
>   Follows the multitude : the yellow solan,
>   Stooping full frequent from his path aloft
>   On his defenceless prey, give presage sure
>   Of the long-wished-for, happy herring drave."

So overwhelming was the spoil from the Auld Haikes, that,
according to him—

> " Auld wives' tub or maister can was crammed,
>   Till Darsie swore, by George, he'd cure no more,
>   And Roger sickened at the smell of herrings."

And not only so, but the very cats were satiated, for
" Even Anst'er tabbies, that were wont to felch
     Herring or haddock rizzering on wall,
     Would at the frying-pan mew, and puff, and spit ;
     Would arch their backs, and grin with desp'rate teeth,
     And eke with tail enlarged, like brush of fox,
     Scud to the house-top, where enraged they'd sit
     Till breakfast or till dinner hour was past,
     And smell of herrings vexed the house no more."

As before the drave became the El Dorado by sea and shore,
the tradesman left his bench or his stool to share the midnight
toil and the midnight prize of the hardy fishers on the deep ;
and the merchant also left counter or desk to invest his capital
and credit in the great silver mine. Season after season
saw it prosper, till 1822, when the following anecdote
will give a suggestive insight into the men and manners
of the day :—Amongst the herring curers that Lammas
on Anstruther shore were the town-clerk, the inn-keeper,
and the young draper, just from Leven. Each had his
little magazine of salt and barrels with a cooper, and the
preparations were not in vain. The harvest came, and as the
most advised market the three friends united with Mr George
Forbes, originally from Elie, but now a leading fish merchant
in Anstruther, to send a cargo to Dublin. Mr Forbes acted
as supercargo, and on his return the joint-stock concern, so to
speak, met in the parlour of Mr Laing's inn to discuss the
balance sheet. The returns just saved a loss. The town-
clerk suggested, and the inn-keeper agreed with him, that
there might be better luck next year ; but the young draper,
Mr Murray, was decided. " No, no," said he, " if herrings at
four shillings or five shillings a cran will not pay, I at least
have done with the trade now and for ever." Next year the
shoals again disappeared from the Forth. ".It's the steam-boats;

E

there's nae doubt about it," cried the wise, as they pointed to the clumsy paddle steamers running between Newhaven and the Tay or the Dee. " Na, na," quoth others, " it was the ringing o' Kingsbarns bell. Wha ever heard o' herrin' in the Auld Haikes after a Sabbath day ?" " People only see the surface, let us tell them," said one oracle, with a look of mingled contempt and pity ; " we told what would happen the first day the herrings were driven to the fields." According to such seers, it was a direct judgment from heaven—more herrings being caught in September of 1822 than could be cured or consumed ; but thus early there were those who held the sea-exhausted theory, of which so much has since been heard from the parlour or the garret in recent years.

CHAPTER XI.

THE MARTYRS TO DUTY, AND THE LOSSES OF FIFTY YEARS AGO.

In the meantime, however, a touching calamity had befallen the homes of Cellardyke. It was on a sunny afternoon in the year 1819. The farmer and his children turned from the green fields to the green sea to watch the boats dancing so gaily on the homeward tack. Two boats in particular are coursing like things of life on the beautiful waters, when one, like a strong foot caught in the race, is borne down by the treacherous white squall. " God help that poor crew," cried the spectators; but within the very brink of destruction the boat righted and is safe. Not so her companion. It is the " Flora," with Alexander Parker as skipper, and, being to leeward, her crew so far had been warned. The sheets are loose, but the hurricane has claimed its victim, and the men have only time—some to cut away a bladder and others to seize, perhaps, a kit, and thus to leap from the gunwale when the wreck, with a long lurch, sinks like a stone to the bottom. The windward boat is flying to the rescue, but seven instead of eight brave men are breasting towards her. One by one they are taken on board; but what of the missing one. It is Alexander Watson, one of the best beloved youths of Cellardyke, last seen as if asleep in the afterhold, which has now become his coffin and his grave. The rescue boat, with the melancholy tale, is steered for Anstruther pier; but sad tidings travel swiftly, and hurried whispers are on every threshold. " Wha is't; wha's droon'd," asks the unfortunate mother, seeing the dejection and sorrow in every face; but

brave men, whose eye never quailed in the battle and the
storm, now steal past bent and broken, till a landsman rudely
unclasps all mystery. " Gang awa hame, woman; it's yer ain
son !"   The disaster occurred on Monday, and on the previous
Sabbath Alexander Watson seemed to lead the young
enquirers who, after earnest study and prayer, were to sit
down at the communion table at its first dispensation by the
popular minister, James Brown, who never forgot the interest
and devotion of one thus early gathered in the harvest of God.
Our narrative of bereavement and sorrow has its next scene
not on the green shores of Fife, but on the stormy coast of
Buchan.   The incident at the time thrilled the heart of the
nation ; but the story is best told in the interesting letter
which an eye-witness sent to the venerable father of the
hero who gave his life with such willing sacrifice to the cause
of humanity :—

FRASERBURGH, 29th January 1822.

DEAR SIR,—With extreme sorrow I write you these lines to
inform you of the death of your son John, which happened on
the 25th day of the month, about four o'clock in the afternoon.
The circumstances attending his death have been truly melancholy for many individuals of this and other places, and has
involved families in the most agonising thoughts and reflections.
The sloop " Mary," of Gardenstown, came in sight of this place
between two and three o'clock of the afternoon of that much-to-
be-lamented day, and soon after made for the harbour, and a
boat in which were six people.   Pilots belonging to this place
went out of the harbour to give what assistance they could.
Two other boats soon followed to act as occasion might require.
The ship came towards the harbour without any apparent danger,
but before the anchor could be let go to bring the vessel up, she
drove, and after it was gone she still drove until she came stern
upon a rock called Baich Head, to the southward of the harbour,

which rock is about 240 yards distant from the harbour. In a few minutes after the vessel struck, one of the boats was upset in the act of attempting to get a line from the vessel to the pier, when five men were immediately engulphed in the merciless waves. The other two boats, after making several dangerous although unsuccessful attempts to obtain possession of the line, were obliged to desist and return to the harbour. On the first boat being upset, the Life-boat was immediately launched into the water, in order to preserve some of the men who were then floating ; but owing to the irresistible fury of the wind and waves, which were still increasing, they were drove ashore on the sands a considerable way from the place where they went out, without being able to give the least assistance. At this melancholy crisis Lieut. Crocker, commanding the boat employed on the Preventive Service here, proposed to attempt to rescue the crew, and one of the pilots was on board the vessel, which had by this time nearly become a perfect wreck, if his crew would assist him in the humane attempt. Accordingly, one of the Preventive boats was launched, in which were Mr Crocker, your son, and two more of the Preventive crew, and a seaman belonging to this place, who proceeded to and reached the wreck in safety ; and the crew of the vessel and pilot were taken from the wreck into the boat, and were in the act of proceeding to the shore when a tremendous sea broke over the vessel and filled the boat—which immediately rendered all human efforts unavailing —and in a few minutes the whole of the unfortunate people were left to the mercy of the waves, and out of the ship's company, boat's crew, and pilot who was on board at the time, none have been spared to relate the melancholy tale but Lieut. Henry Crocker, who, being a good swimmer and being lightly dressed, and having had presence of mind to divest himself of the coat he had on at the time, his hat, and neckcloth, was a great means in the hand of Providence in saving him. This is the most accurate and true account I can give you of the sad catastrophe that has happened, which will be long remembered and severely felt in this place. My brother-in-law, whom you knew, was the unfortunate pilot who suffered along with your son ; and had it not been that I was taken up so much in soothing the mind of his unfortunate widow, I would have wrote you sooner. Your son's corpse came on shore yesterday morning, and is to be interred in this church-yard this day at three o'clock afternoon. I need not give you any directions about how you shall inform your son's widow of her loss. May God enable you to put up with what I have related to you, and to communicate to her in a suitable manner the melancholy news. You may acquaint my friend, David Watson, and friends what I have said, and may God enable you and your connections to bow with Christian fortitude and resignation to the Divine Will ; and may He be pleased to direct and protect each of us in our several occupations through life, is the wish of your afflicted but sincere friend,

ALEXANDER NOBLE JOSEPH.

This martyr to duty is commemorated in a fine obelisk in Kilrenny Churchyard, placed over the grave of his widow, Margaret Lothian, who survived till the 25th of December 1859, by their only child, John Martin, Esq. of St Ayles' Crescent—the thrice elected Provost of the burgh—and whose name has also been for years as familiar as a household word in connection with the oil-cloth manufacture of Cellardyke.

Time rolls on, and the cry—the piercing cry of the widow and the orphan—is again heard on the shores. It is a bleak day in the spring of 1826, when, let us observe, the deep sea going boats of Cellardyke have far outgrown its little harbour. The moorings are in three tiers, by as many stout chains, which have replaced the thigh-thick cables of an earlier day. The enterprise of the coast, however, is not arrested by such an obstacle, and the dashing new boat which has engrossed so much attention as she rose plank and plank under the hands of the old wright, James Henderson, at Anstruther Brae, now counts the four-and-twentieth of the fleet. She is named the " Victory," and is owned in shares, which is still the rule on the coast, and, being her maiden voyage, no little interest is of course felt to know how she will work at sea. Perhaps she is a little crank under the mainsail, but still the crew are proud of their gallant boat, and all goes well till, on the voyage home, they encounter the dreadful storm which swept over the coast on Thursday, the 6th of April. A brave hand was at the helm ; but the black squall laughs at all precautions, and, reeling like a stricken bird on the pathway of destruction, the ill-fated boat is next instant engulphed in the angry waves. Once a wild cry rises through the crash of the tempest ; but never again so swiftly did seven gallant mariners sink into a watery grave. One, however, is left to battle with the storm, all alone—no friendly eye, no friendly ear to catch, perchance, the death cry. Oh ! the suspense, the agony of such a situation— every wave rushing on with the menace or the message of death ; but the arm of heaven is around him, till, at the end of more than an hour, he is seen and rescued by his neighbours in the boat " Johns," of Cellardyke. The disaster occurred in the afternoon, about four miles to the eastward of the Island of May, and the sufferers are as follows :—David Taylor, sen. ; David Taylor, jun. ; William Taylor, Robert Pratt, William Peattie, Andrew Heugh, Robert Corstorphine. The survivor is William Pratt, a son of old Alexander, the daring sailor of the war. An Edinburgh newspaper of the day says :—" By this calamitous event, four poor widows and a number of helpless children totally unprovided for, are left to bewail the loss of their husbands and fathers. Two of the persons who have suffered were lately married, and their

widows are pregnant.   Such as were unmarried were the
support of aged parents, or of younger brothers and sisters.
In short, each of these poor mourning families have a claim
on the sympathy of the humane; but upon one family the
stroke has fallen with peculiar severity : a father and his two
sons are among the deceased.   The 'Victory' was thirty-four
feet long, but in her day she was regarded as a floating
leviathian, and the flush of pride was on manly faces when she
first kissed the brine.   One of these, and also one of her
owners, was Andrew Heugh, a brother of Captain Walter
Heugh, so widely known in reference to the Wallaroo copper
mines.   The family was originally from Pittenweem, but the
' Preventive man' duties of the father had brought them to
Cellardyke, where Andrew married and settled as a fisherman,
while Captain Hughes began in 1818 his apprenticeship in
Mr Sharp's curing yard as a cooper, which he quitted after a
rather unlucky venture on his own account at Crail, to begin
that romantic career first as a sailor, then as a sheep farmer,
and next, by a happy chance, the master of an Australian
copper field, which has placed him amongst the most successful
men of his time."   Ten months had not elapsed when " There
is sorrow on the sea ; it cannot be quiet," was again the
mournful text of an East of Fife pulpit. It referred to Saturday,
the 11th of February 1828.   The mourners were assembling.
Here the old elder, pale and withered like the last sheaf in
autumn ; there the young student, full of the hopes and
aspirations which his bright eye cannot conceal ; this the
owner of broad lands and that the toiler with the one thread-
bare coat—all side by side to bear the remains of the sainted
mother of Thomas Chalmers to the grave.   It is a memorable
day in Anstruther, and none the less so for the fearful blast
of wind and snow and hail, which at the moment the bearers

stoop to lift their solemn burthen sends the stoutest reeling
to the wall. It roars like thunder over the house tops, and
the bewildered wife, turning to the dark sea, beaten like chaff
by the wing of the tempest, prays in her agony—" God in
His mercy help them on the water in an hour like this."
Such was the conflict in which a little sail was seen to engage
in Largo Bay ; but it was short and decisive. That boat was
never seen more. The sequel is soon told. It was the stout
little drave boat returning down the Forth with staves to
Anstruther, when there and then all on board met a watery
grave—these being Andrew Crawford, the skipper ; James
Budge, of the little drug shop on the shore ; Peter Watson,
weaver ; and John Philp, wheelwright. The skipper was a
native of Cellardyke, but, like his three companions, he
had his home at this time in Anstruther, where they
left widows, and in nearly every case children likewise
more or less unable, as the phrase went, " to fend for
themselves." These were, in truth, evil days for the Fife
coast, for only next year the streets of Cellardyke were once
more saddened by wives and children weeping for their
beloved, never, never to return again. It happened on the
24th of September 1828, when the white fishing fleet, as
before the loss of the " Victory," was reckoned at twenty-four
boats. The crews were also still in the custom of concluding
the drave, or rather of proceeding the lines by a trip to the
mussel beds of the Eden in order to lay up a bait provision
for the winter, and this day several coast boats were lying
deeply laden in the river, where the rule of the old tacksman,
Arthur Berrie, was " Fill your bait, men ; but tak' little or
tak' muckle, you've fifteen pound to gi'e me." The tide was
on the bar, but the heavens were dark with the west wind, and
the old fishers advised, though the young men grumbled, to

come to anchor for the night. A Cellardyke boat, however,
is pushed into the stream. "There's David Roger, if it's
weather for him it's weather for us," cried the skipper's son of
the "Olive." John Davidson shakes his head, but youth is
resolute and strong, and another boat is soon breasting to sea.
With the cliffs of St Andrews to windward all is perhaps well
but rounding the Carr and full in the Forth, and so at the mercy
of the tempest. "Can they escape?" The windward boat
anticipates the danger. "Let's into Fifeness and lighten her,"
said the skipper, and the order once executed she is bounding
on her stormy way, like one relieved of a deadly burthen.
The expedient, however, is all unobserved and unheeded by
the "Olive," which again, as if by a fatal temptation, follows
in the race. And gallantly she does so—tack for tack—till
not three furlongs from Crail harbour she staggers headlong,
like a wrestler in the fight, and so it is now with death and
despair, for within the breath she is over-mastered and sinking
in the breakers. Seven brave men are seen on the gunwale,
but with six the glass is run. Amongst these is the skipper
and his son. "James," said the veteran in the tenderness
of the last farewell. "Father," answers the young man with
the same look of melting love and confidence, and then clasped
to each other's bosom they sink without a struggle into the
raging flood. And thus all alone the oldest and most
enfeebled man in the boat sees the last agony of his own two
sons, his brother and that brother's son who are amongst the
six that perish ; but he holds on, and on to his frail stay, a
drifting kit, till at last, just as his grasp is loosening in the
dreadful conflict, he is caught by a friendly hand, and is
saved in one of the boats that observed the tragedy. The
survivor is William Davidson—the sufferers being the skipper,
John Davidson, who left a wife and daughter ; and his son

James, who had been but a short time married; William's two sons: William and Andrew, unmarried. The bodies of the skipper and his son, who perished in each other's arms, were cast up by the sea at Arbroath three weeks after the catastrophe. They would appear to have been locked in that last loving embrace almost to the hour they were found, as a rock only lay between parent and child, who rest in one grave under the shadows of the grand old sanctuary of St Vigeans. Young William Davidson's body was found floating at sea, and so landed by one of the Cellardyke boats. We extract the following reference to the calamity from a Fife paper of the day :—" A society was established in Anstruther about two years and a-half ago, called the Caledonian Gardener Society. Upon the death of any of its members the Society pays the widow or nearest relative of the deceased £5 as funeral money, besides other provisions. In the Cellardyke boat that was lost last week not less than four of its members perished, and a day or two before an account has arrived of the death of one of its members in the East Indies, a most promising young man, a captain of a vessel, who has left a widow and three children to lament his loss, being in all five members in one week. It was truly gratifying, at a meeting of the Society on Monday night, to see the spirit of philanthropy displayed by every member vieing with each other who should first pay their quota of said funeral money. This Society has really done much good in its way, and ought to be encouraged, particularly by seafaring people, as it has paid not less than 11 to 12 funerals, amounting to about £55 or £60, since its establishment, all of which have been (with one exception) premature deaths. In the last Cellardyke boat that was lost previous to this three members were drowned, and in the one belonging to this place, lost last year in Largo Bay, one member was drowned."

The following year has also a place in the melancholy register of loss at sea. The Anstruther sailors and tradesmen had, in the spirit of their forefathers, fitted out three drave boats, long famous as the red, the white, and the black tankards. The last of these, the "Magdalene," was fishing that Lammas at Fraserburgh, with honest old David Grubb as the skipper, when one dark night, as she was swinging at the drift, her bows were crushed in by a north country boat, which completed the cruel outrage by stealing away and leaving the Anstruther crew without one word of pity to their fate. The skipper had scarcely time to warn his companions to seize the first float or spar which came to their hand, when the old tankard gave a long lurch and sank under their feet. They all rose to the surface, however, except a hapless young man, married but a few months before, belonging to St Andrews, who perished with the boat. The sea was crowded with fishing craft; but, unseen and unheard in the darkness, the poor castaways had to buffet for an hour or more with the waves before relief came. The exhaustion and anxiety of that night, however, were too much for the veteran skipper, who sank into a premature grave.

CHAPTER XII.

THE STORY OF THE WINTER DRAVE—HERRING ADVENTURES AND THE WRECK AT THE MAY.

Happier days were in store, and in the interval a new fishery, like a new and richer mine, was opened, so as to make hope and confidence once more sparkle in every eye. We refer to the winter drave. In one sense it was no discovery ; the Monks of the May knew, and fished the herrings for ling and kellin bait. It was the same errand that led, as we saw, to the catastrophe at Cellardyke in 1800 ; but it was the conviction of the old fathers that their single chance was to anchor the net in some secluded inlet or bay, where, like the sea trout, the shoals would hover in the mystery of their birth. So it had been, and so it was likely to be, till one night, as the " Box Harry," of Cellardyke, was bound on the usual errand, the signs of herring life in the offing were so singular and decided as to induce the old skipper, Alexander Cunningham, to exclaim—" Men, what do you to say to shoot ?" The idea of casting the nets for herring in such a situation was so fantastic that his son could only laugh. " Just as weel dae that, faither, in Renny Hill Park," and, wrapping his jacket round his head, went to sleep between the timbers—then the fishers' only midnight couch—but the old skipper was not to be dissuaded, and, with the assistance of the rest of the crew, the drift was cast into the witching sea. It was an interesting experiment, and curiosity was on tip-toe to catch the result. Nor was she disappointed ; for, drawing the rope, the lug of the first net was shining like silver with the scally treasure. Old Saunders

was in ecstacies. " Clash them in the lubber's chafts, Tam,"
he cried, throwing up a handful of herrings. It was the signal
for active work, and the success of that night gave, as we
shall see, a new and brighter turn to the destinies of the shore.

Another incident, no less romantic, enriched the harvest,
and may also be regarded as the birth of one of the leading
industries of recent times. Red herrings hung for days in the
kiln were familiar on the coast ; but the Anstruther cooper—
Andrew Innes—was the first to glean the secret of the rich
and delicate " bloater," which he did from a grateful English-
man in the harbour of Peterhead. The cooper was not the
man to lose a chance for his master, Bailie George Darsie, and,
hearing that the Pittenweem boats had, the year after the
adventure of the "Box Harry," fallen in with a large shoal in the
Forth, he travelled west and purchased right and left at five-
and-twenty shillings a barrel. " What's the news at Pittenweem, this mornin' ?" asked the gracious old Bailie, standing
in his own door, at a sedate fish merchant of the sister burgh.
" News, Bailie ! Weel may ye speer, Bailie. Yer man has
bocht forty barrel o' herrin', and the price is naething less—
no a penny less—than five-and-twenty shillin's a barrel."
" Is he drunk or daft," exclaimed the perplexed Magistrate,
who could not conceal his anger and surprise, which had not
left him when his trusty overseer came to report the transactions of the morning. " A foolish thing, Andrew, man ; a
foolish thing," and refusing his countenance, the master in-
dignantly turned away ; but, full of his project, the cooper
hastened to the herring yard to put his kilns in order, and
the first Packet that sailed carried the first Anstruther
bloaters for shipment with the Leith and London steamers.
" Yer bloaters ha'e turned the penny, Andrew. " I never did
sae weel wi' naething before," said the Bailie, radiant as a

May morning, as he glanced over the sales about a week later.
The herrings had actually realised forty-seven shillings a
barrel in Billingsgate ; and need we say that " Try again "
became the order of the day, as indeed it has ever been the
watchword of the fishing trade. The herrings were bought on
the 9th of February 1827, and the Pittenweem crews continued
the fishery with great spirit and general success till they were
overtaken by an unparalleled disaster on Wednesday, the
20th of February 1833. The herrings were on the coast, and,
full of hope and rejoicing in the singular mildness of the day,
the crews had sped betimes to sea. They had cast and even
drawn their nets, some with four or six and even eight crans,
but by midnight the estuary was wrapt in one of the most
dreadful storms that ever rolled across the German sea. The
boats, in the first hours of the storm, ran into Elie harbour,
and others, in the last extremity, found shelter in Cocklemill
burn, but three boats belonging to Pittenweem, and one to
St Monance, perished in the gale. One of the Pittenweem
boats struck on the rock at the entrance to the west harbour,
when one man, Robert Adamson, escaped to the shore, but
his companions, with their death cry ringing in the ears of
wife and children, met a watery grave. This was the " Helen"
and " Robert," owned by the skipper, George Horsburgh, who
was lost with three of his crew. The other boats were the
" Rising Suns," which swamped in deep water, though neither
Skipper Duncan nor any of his four companions were spared
to tell the tale, and the " Peace and Unity," which was
cast ashore keel up on Elie beach, her crew of five men, including Skipper Bridges, having also perished. A similar
fate overtook Alexander Reekie and his crew—five in all— of
the St Monance boat, which was seen drifting in the same
melancholy situation as the last in the stormy offing. The

total loss was nineteen fishermen ; but the public sympathy
rose to the calamity, and a relief fund having been organised
by Andrew Johnstone, M.P., Sir Ralph Anstruther, and
Colonel Lindsay, about £2000 were collected for the widows
and the fatherless. In those years was seen for the first
time the broad contrast which has so often existed since
between the old enterprise and the new—that is, the herring
fishery of spring and the herring fishery of Lammas—the one
spreading out like a forest tree, but the other once and
again not more than a shadow of the past. We refer, of
course, to the Forth, for season by season the coast was sending a larger fleet to Caithness and Peterhead, though at home
it actually seemed, as the Fife chronicler had said two centuries before, that " there was to be no drave hereafter."
But here is an old herring fisher to speak for himself. It is
James Lindsay, so famous in Edinburgh University as Sir
John Leslie's man. The season was 1826, when the philoso-
pher, as his neighbours called him, was a boat mate with
Bailie Crawford and four others. For a month and a day
they toiled night after night and caught nothing ; but the
cry of herrings at Dunbar sent them scudding to the southward, though there only to learn that the shoal was at Holy
Island, for which it was next resolved to tack and steer.
Here they found the sloop " Williams," of Crail, with Andrew
Innes as supercargo, waiting, but waiting in vain, for their
own errand, till one day advices came of herrings at Stonehaven, for which sloop and boat were that very tide under-
way. Again, however, it was " a wild goose chase," and the
end of the forlorn season saw them " settling up " in John
Wilson's public-house on the shore of Cellardyke. It had
been truly a luckless venture, for instead of a profit each man
was seven shillings in debt, and, as may be supposed, more

was felt than said, till the father of the company, John Reid, old and lame as he was, sprang to his feet, " I've seen a' this afore," cried the veteran, " we'll ha'e gude fortune yet, brithers—half-a-mutchkin on the head o't." The advice, need we say, was taken, but many a day, notwithstanding, the home fisher toiled on a fruitless sea. Brighter times, however, dawned at last, though, as so often happens, the watchers are asleep at the opening gate. The shoals return as mysteriously as they went, and no one suspected that herrings were on the shore, till a lovely September day in 1836 two urchins—George Barclay and David Roger—came racing in from the hand lines with the joyful cry that " living herring in the cod's mooth." That night the old Dyker yawl, with a volunteer crew and a volunteer skipper in our old friend James Lindsay, set ten herring nets in the offing, and came in next morning with six, on the morrow with eight, and on the third day with twenty barrels. The news flew along the coast as if it had been rung out from the steeples, and boats gathered in like sea birds to the banquet. But a sudden storm ended the season, though not before new plans and new resolutions were taken for the next. In 1836 the Cellardyke fleet fished in the north, with the exception of four reserved crews, who divided the season between the Forth and Holy Island, but in the following year instead of four there were forty boats at home—the success being so remarkable that four hundred barrels are estimated as the average of the hundred boats on the Fife coast. The usual selling price of the cure was twenty-two shillings a barrel, so that in official circles it was stated and believed that the value of the harvest was not less than £41,000. The coast wakened up in a day from the apathy and slumber of years—the dry sands are once more singing in the sunlight ; but we cannot forget the appalling

F

catastrophe which plunged the shore into mourning, and that on the gladsome harvest eve. The sorrow of the sea has indeed few more affecting incidents than the wreck of the excursion boat at the Isle of May on Saturday, the 1st July 1837, when so many sweet young lives were whirled like a leaf on the blast, from the scene of revelry and mirth, into the solemn secrets of the grave.

It was no new adventure that fatal sail; on the contrary, it was a time-honoured custom of the shore to launch the drave boat, and give friends and neighbours a holiday on that romantic isle. A dance on the May—how young hearts throbbed and fair cheeks flushed with joy at the thought. Even old eyes, dim with years, and it might be with the weariness of the life march, brighten up over the sunny memories of the olden time. Here, then, we have the secret this Saturday morning on the pier of Cellardyke, where as many as five boats are unmooring for the island. All eyes, however, turned towards one, evidently the "Admiral" ship in size and build; but listen, and you can hear the attraction, as it is con-fessed by a ruddy maiden, "Come, Rob, and let's gang wi' the music." Three violins have struck up at the moment, and the "Johns," with her living freight of five-and-sixty souls, is pushed from the pier. It is a summer sky and a summer sea, and the island is reached betimes, and with Kirkonhaven on the lea the boat is steered for the little pier. The breakers, the last echo of the sea winds, are white and booming on the reef; but the oarsmen are young and fearless, and a skilful hand is on the helm, and all goes well. "A good voyage, and a pleasant landing," cries one, and fair hands are busy with shawl and kerchief; but at that very moment a wild plunge and a startled cry betrays the danger— scarcely heard, however, when, with a deafening crash, the doomed boat falls upon the skerry. How changed is now the once joyous scene! All is confusion and terror; the air is rent with shrieks of women and children, who stand the very picture of despair. Still there is a chance; a firm foot can leap the chasm, and brave men are bounding to and fro with precious burthens; but, alas! a panic seized the remnant, who, rushing to the higher gunwale, the boat rolls from her perch, and sinks like a stone in the deep water. It was a fearful scene—a frantic mass of women and children clinging to each other with the grasp of death, struggled in the waves; but the terrible appeal is not in vain. Heroes plunge in to the rescue. " I saw the Kingsbarns sailor, David Spence, bring seven to the shore," said a Cellardyke friend to us. One young fisher had his sister and another dearer still in his arms; but both were lost, and he himself was scarcely saved. Yet after all the gallant deeds that were done thirteen sank to rise no more. The death roll is a sad one. The bereavements in Cellardyke are—Margaret Carstairs, thirteen; Euphemia Stevenson, twelve; and Euphemia Anderson, nine years of age. The others are a fair damsel with rich golden tresses, named Jane Brown, belonging to Kingsbarns, and Isabella, aged twenty, the daughter of James Butters, the foreman of Thirdpart. Anstruther was especially smitten that day—eight of the sufferers being connected with this place, namely, Margaret Taylor, the wife of Captain Sangster, and her sister's child, Magdalene Young; old widow David Wilson, or Mary Bell, as the neighbours would say, and her daughter-in-law, Mary Skinners, the wife of Alexander Wilson, schoolmaster, Radernie, and James, their infant son, nine weeks old. There was also the gentle maiden, Katie Andrews, the orphan child of poverty and talent, with Ann Anderson, scarcely seventeen years, the daughter of the old sheriff-officer; and the

bride-elect, Janet Muir, aged twenty-two, of the household
of Peter Muir, who had another child amongst the rescued
from the wreck.   The scene at Cellardyke pier that Saturday
evening was, indeed, solemn and affecting, nor soon to be forgotten.   It was an awful contrast to the song and dance of
the morning, for now the bodies of the dead, dripping with
the cruel wave, had been landed, and bereaved friends had
come to recognise, or to make enquiries after their own.
Amongst these was Alexander Brown, who chanced, like
hundreds, to be at the draper's sale at Anstruther looking into
the faces of the dead.   " My Jeannie's no there," he said, with
a sigh of relief, as if the next boat would restore his beloved
safe and well to his bosom.   Yet she was in the ghastly train ;
but the old crofter of Kingsbarns is not alone in failing to
realise the once familiar features when written with the secrets
of a watery grave.   A notable incident in point occurred some
fifty years ago on Anstruther beach. A singular character, named
Philip Oliphant, better known as " Cuddie Deil," stung to
despair by age and want, threw himself into the midnight sea
at the back of the old pier.   The lifeless body was found next
morning.   A crowd gathered on the spot, but not one knew
or could name the unhappy victim, till, at the suggestion of
an old sailor, he was lifted to his feet, when a hundred voices
cried in a breath, " Cuddie Deil."   The disaster at the May
was a crushing misfortune to the poor skipper.   He lost his
boat, and not only so, but for more than a year a cruel and
unnecessary prosecution hung over his head.   It devolved
on the late Town-Clerk, M. F. Conolly, at whose instance as
Procurator-Fiscal for the East of Fife, he was apprehended,
but liberated on bail, to answer to a charge of culpable
homicide.   The trial took place before the High Court of
Justiciary on the 15th of March 1838.   He was indicted for

having crowded sixty-five persons into a boat thirty-six feet long and twelve feet two inches wide; with having landed at Kirkonhaven, instead of the stand or the "Altar Stanes;" and with having used four oars instead of six or eight, which, in the prosecutor's view, ought to have been taken to pull the boat through the eddies. "Guilty or not guilty," fixed all eyes on John Sutherland, the panel at the bar. A look of anxious concern shaded his honest brow; but bearing and answer bespoke the innocent man. Evidence was then led— the first witness being Alexander Wood, or "Briton Sandy," whose boat was one of the five that fatal day at the island. He was asked why he on that occasion selected another landing place, and his manly answer exploded the most serious charge against his townsman, "My own pleasure. I might have taken one landing as well as another." The next witness was Robert Davidson, one of the twelve fishermen on board of the "Johns," who aptly explained that though the boat belonged to John Sutherland, yet he had no more interest or responsibility than his eleven companions in the excursion, for which nothing was asked and nothing was paid by the excursionists, who were, moreover, the boatmen's dearest relatives and friends. It fairly broke down the charge, which the Lord-Advocate at once withdrew. The acquittal followed: but the presiding judge warned the fishermen not to take so many passengers in future, a warning, however, which has not since been needed, as with that fatal trip the once favourite holiday was ended.

CHAPTER XIII.

THE REV. GEORGE DICKSON AND THE FISHERIES —THE BLACK DECADE.

The well-remembered minister of the parish, the Rev. George Dickson, wrote about this time an interesting sketch of Cellardyke in connection with the statistical account of Kilrenny. The account includes the census of 1841, when the population had increased from only 1043 in the year 1801 ; from 1233 in 1811 ; from 1494 in 1821 ; from 1705 in 1831, to 2039. Cellardyke at this time had 282 seafaring men, and likewise, according to the returns given in by the schoolmaster, Mr Bonthron, 197 houses, 318 families, and 1486 inhabitants. Mr Dickson quotes the following from the Blue Book on the Scottish burghs :—" That Nether Kilrenny has a harbour for fishing boats, for the improvement of which £1200 were advanced by the Board of Trustees for the improvement of fisheries, and £500 were raised by the town, which have been expended in building new quays ; but they have not been judiciously placed, and the harbour is said to have been rather injured than improved in their erection." For the sake, how- ever, of the venerable writer we give the notice of the sea as it left his pen. Here it is :—" The fishery in Cellardyke is carried on to a very great extent. The fishermen are active, hardy, and enterprising, and prosecute their lawful employ- ment oftentimes under circumstances of great danger. There are about 100 large boats, varying in tonnage from 13 to 18 tons, employed during the summer season in the herring fishery, each of these being manned with three or four regular fishermen, and one or two half-dealsmen, as they are called, who have no nets, but merely assist in rowing and hauling the nets ; or if they have not the full complement of men two or three strong boys are sometimes taken. It was the usual practice for the whole of the fishermen to go to Peterhead and Wick to prosecute the fishing, without a single boat being left to try if herring could be got in the Firth of Forth ; but in 1837 or 1838 some of the fishermen remained at home, and were very successful, and since that period a great number of boats have been employed at home with various success, and during some seasons have been more successful than those which went to the north. At times the boats were brought into the harbour with from forty to eighty crans ; but when the herrings are so abundant the fishery continues only for a few days. When the fishermen get 200 crans they account such a fair fishing ; but many do not attain to that number. During a successful fishing season lately one or two boats got about 400 crans or barrels, and it is believed that one caught the extraordinary number of 500 crans. Their agreement with the curers is generally from nine shillings to eleven shillings per cran, with a certain allowance of whisky. It is not, however, all gain that is made by the fishing, as it is attended with very considerable expense. The boats, when thoroughly fitted for going to sea, cost about £100, and require a considerable sum to keep them in repair, while the nets, when ready for use, cost about five pounds each, and the number taken by each boat varies from fourteen to twenty. The herring fishing is prosecuted for a short time in winter, during the months of January and February, and in autumn during the months of August and September. The other months are occupied by the fishermen in prosecuting the white fishing, when 28 or 30 boats go regularly to sea every morning if the weather permits, and proceed oftentimes to the distance of 40 or 50 miles in search of fish. The boats in these cases are manned with eight men each, and while each man furnishes a certain portion of line, with the necessary hooks attached, the produce is equally divided among the fishermen, the owner of the boat being entitled to a double share. In this mode of fishing a considerable expense is also incurred, both in the purchase of mussels for bait, which are generally brought from the Eden beyond St Andrews, and also by the frequent loss of their fishing tackle. In summer the fish are generally taken to Fisherrow and Newhaven, or to Dundee and Perth, and in winter they are generally brought into the harbour, and sold to the fishcurers or to the cadgers, who cart them to a great distance, and dispose of them in the different towns throughout. The fishcurers smoke the haddocks and pickle the cod which they purchase, and send to the Glasgow, Liverpool, and London markets. Besides the fishermen who are engaged in the fishing, the means of subsistence are afforded to a number of other individuals, such as coopers, carters, and women, who are employed in cleaning and curing the fish. It would be difficult to ascertain the amount of money which is brought in from the deep in the course of a year; but estimating each fishing boat at 120 crans on an average in ordinary years, the sum realised at 10s per crans would amount to £6000, besides the profits arising from the takes of cod and haddocks during the summer season, which is very considerable; but when the expense of keeping up these lines, and the payment of their bait, are taken into consideration, these apparent gains are much diminished. A cartload of mussels brought from the Eden costs from twenty shillings to thirty-two shillings, and the lines which are employed in fishing by each fisherman extend to 1800 feet in winter, and double that length in summer, so that when the whole or even a portion of the line is lost a considerable sum is necessary to repair the deficiency. Many of the fishermen are in respectable circumstances, and careful in the management of their substance; but it is matter of deep regret that the same cannot be said of all of them. Mrs D. Bethune, as the superior, is entitled to every fourteenth fish of the different kinds, with the exception of herring, of which she has a right to every eighteenth; but instead of exacting the rent in fish an agreement has been entered into with the fishermen, by which they consent, in lieu of the fish, to pay £40 annually. As the harbour is intended merely for fishing boats, no ships or foreign vessels are allowed to enter it." Such was our old sea home when it was overtaken not by one but by a series of disasters, which make the next seven years the darkest in the annals of the coast. The first occurred during the dreadful gale from the westward on Tuesday, the 29th of March 1842. Many an anxious eye was turned that day towards the North Sea, as the billows, like warriors waving their white plumes, rushed to the conflict with the howling tempest; and well might mothers and sisters weep for the brave men exposed to the wrath of the pitiless storm. The fishing boats were at sea, but one by one they gallantly breasted the raging west. Now on the port, now on the starboard tack and all went well, till in a fatal moment one luckless craft, the "Lord Melbourne," just as she had rounded in the wind's eye, but before the ballast could be trimmed, is struck by a dreadful squall. It was an evil moment for the death wrestle. Helpless and unprepared the boat sinks before the destroyer, and seven gallant men have looked their last on sea and sky. They perished, but not without a struggle, as men struggle for life, and all that makes life sweet and lovely —for home, for children—yet all was in vain; and now, like the last two disasters, one solitary man is left to fight the awful conflict, when his companions are one by one gone by his side. He would have shared their fate ; but in a fortunate moment he clutched some bladders or buoys, which proved to him the ark of life, till he was rescued by the boat "Sovereign," of Cellardyke, which bore down to his relief. The survivor was James Dickson, whose story, as we shall see, is a sad and touching one. The sufferers were—the skipper and owner, Henry Reid, unmarried ; Adam Reid, left a widow and three children ; William Reid, left a widow ; James Meldrum, a native of St Monance, but married and settled in Cellardyke, left a widow and five children ; William Robertson, left a widow and three children, besides a son, William, who perished with his father on that fatal forenoon ; Andrew Anderson, a native of Queensferry, and a son of the old fish trader already referred to, left a widow and two children. The skipper and his brothers, Adam and William, perished side by side ; but the fate of William Robertson and his son is amongst the most touching incidents of the sea. When the boat was struck by the squall, and all was lost, the young man, less perhaps in terror than in the pathos of the last farewell of life and love, gave way to a burst of tears, when his father quitted his hold on the mast, and clasped him to his bosom, saying, " Dinna be fear'd, Willie, yer faither's gaun wi' ye," and so they sank into a watery grave.

> " Alas ! for love, if thou were't all,
> And nought beyond, O, death."

The next disaster was little more than two years later. It happened on the 16th of May 1844. During the day the weather had been singularly soft and sultry, with a sickly south wind, ever struggling, ever beaten as if by some strong but secret enemy, which in the meantime has been gathering and marshalling his squadrons for the onslaught, and then

> " Colder and louder blew the wind,
>   A gale from the north-east ;
> The snow fell hissing in the brine,
>   And the billows frothed like yeast."

An old fisher near the Urquhart Wynd had a quaint but expressive way of picturing this deceitful weather. " It's a butter melter the noo," he would say, wiping his honest brow ; " but look oot for the tarry freezer the nicht." The deep sea going boats of Cellardyke, however, true to the intrepid character of the shore, were ploughing in the light of the evening stars, some homeward, but more outward bound ; indeed, it seemed, as so often happens in a Scottish spring, that " all signs had failed," and that the summer had already come to gladden sea and shore. Such were the feelings of the hour when a little squadron of Cellardyke hoisted sail for the deep sea. One of the boats, named the " William," was gallantly dashing through the deepening gloom, foresail and mainsail set full to the breeze, and with a young but kindly hand upon the helm, when last seen, or at least recognised by some neighbours, who were themselves all but overwhelmed within the hour by the terrific whirlwind, on which, as it rushed past, death and destruction seemed to sit as charioteers. It was midnight, and the Bell light flickered faintly through the driving storm, " when, was it the shriek of the wild winds or the cry of drowning men ?" no one could tell. It came and went so swiftly on the startled ear, but that gallant boat returned no more. The sea holds the secret —the sad secret—over which wives and children wept so many days ; but the whisper was only too fearfully realised that the boat had gone down in the midnight squall. The eight sufferers were—the skipper and owner, George Smith, who left a widow and three children ; James Smith, his brother, who was also a married man, with five children, his son George being one of the hapless crew ; James Forrester Watson, who left a widow and seven orphans ; John Sutherland, whose young widow bore her son six months after his father was sleeping in the waves ; Wilson Brunton, who had but lately taken to sea life, left a widow and four orphans in helpless childhood ; James Salter, a native of Kilrenny, who left a widow and one child ; Robert Mackay, a young unmarried man, from Sutherlandshire.   The third calamity occurred within the second year, being on the night of Tuesday, the 23d of April 1846.   The circumstances bear a painful resemblance to the former catastrophe—indeed, the one is almost a shadow of the other, for here again the gallant new boat, the " Nancy," is last seen dashing through the midnight waves.   She had all sails set, and was cleaving her path in foam and spray, and so flitted away till she was lost in the shadows of the midnight, where the old fishers believe she was caught like a bird on the wing by the dreadful hurricane, which, as before, swept from the stormy North. Next day many an eye was turned to the stormy main, but it was only to watch and weep ; the stately boat never came back again, and, like his three brothers but four years byegone, the skipper and his six companions lay in a watery grave.   It was a surmise at the time that the " Nancy " was swamped about five leagues to the eastward of the May, but on such occasions rumour, like the sea bubble, is only a child of the air.   The names of the crew who perished that night, with the particulars of the widows and orphans, are as follows : —Thomas Reid, master, a widow and five children ; William Muir, a widow and four children ; Thomas Muir, a widow and two children ; George Anderson, a widow and two children ;

John Wilson, a widow and two children; Alexander Wilson, a widow and a daughter, not born, however, till many weeks after the loss; John Boyter, unmarried, but the last support of his aged mother. The eighth man of the crew, Andrew Wilson, chanced to be on shore that night, in consequence of a sore hand, and thus escaped the fate of his brothers, John and Alexander. The following lines were written, it is said, at the time by a ploughboy on the farm of Caiplie, and were prised in the hour of distress far above more elegant compositions, and so we here give them a place—

" You fishermen of Cellardyke, that on the sea do sail,
Come listen with attention unto this mournful tale,
It's of a splendid new boat—the " Nancy "—lost at sea,
With seven of a crew, my boys, the truth I'll tell to you.
On the twenty-second of April, a dark and misty night,
She sailed out of Anst'er pier at ten o'clock at night;
She steered her course to the eastward of the May,
And there, they say, she did go down, when fifteen miles away.

O! these poor and humble fishermen all meet a watery grave,
Without an eye to pity them, or yet an arm to save;
Nor was there any present their hurried death to prove;
But we hope they all have landed in that happy home above.
Six widows they have left behind, and fifteen children dear,
For to lament the loss of them that on the seas did steer;
Oh! Providence, be kind to them, and good unto them prove,
Guide them and protect them all with thy sovereign love.

You, brethren, join in unity, and show your liberal hand,
And let the harvest season do all the good it can
For to maintain their widows, who are now so bereft,
Likewise their orphan children, who fatherless are left;
Rear you up their children unto some future stage,
And then they will remember you when once they come of age.

I must conclude, and make an end, and finish out my lines;
I hope it will give no offence to whom it does belong.
Although I am a ploughman's boy I feel for others too;
Now I have got no more to say—I bid you all adieu !"

The fourth of these terrible catastrophes, which occurred on the morning of Tuesday, the 3d of November 1848, had in some touching particulars a mystery and pathos all its own. In those years, indeed, a strange fatality seemed to hang about the deep sea fleet of Cellardyke. " I remember," said a grey-haired father on the bulwark, " when the boats were long reckoned at four-and-twenty." Another launch, another loss ; but it happened again, some thirteen or fourteen years later, when the four crews suffered, and turned the count as often back to twenty-nine or thirty. Such was the muster on Cellardyke pier that morning— a morning so dark that a crew actually boarded their neighbour's boat for their own, and had the sails rigged before realising the mistake. Two had just chimed when one gallant boat after another pushed out to " veer and tack" in the rising sea wind, and anon through the driving mist and rain. Weathering the Island of May, however, the fleet encountered the full sweep of the gale, and boat after boat bore up for the friendly shore. Others continued the conflict in all the dashing spirit of the sea—

> "Oh ! who can tell, save he whose heart hath tried,
> And danced in triumph o'er the waters wide,
> The exulting sense, the pulse's maddening play,
> That thrills the wanderer of that trackless way ?"

The most fearless, however, gave up the endeavour to cast hook and line, and sooner or later fled from the storm ; but that night there was one brave crew the less in the dear old home. It was the " Johns and Mary," of whom no tidings could be heard, save the short and hurried whisper which passed from lip to lip in the twilight, the import of which was but too easily read in the hushed voice and dejected face. The gale and the waves were raging high ; but in neither lay the dreadful secret which that midnight rent the air with the widows' cry. The rumour ran, and none might doubt it, that one of the Baltic fleet, a large brig under close reefed topsails, bearing up like the fishing fleet before the storm had dealt the fatal blow, which sent boat and crew to the bottom. The scene was believed to be a league to the south-east of the Isle of May, where—oh, sadly true of many a sea hero of Fife—

> " The ocean is a mighty grave,
> Its breast a burial ground ;
> And every little swelling wave
> Is but a graveyard mound."

That very morning two oars, a broken plank, and three or four line baskets and other apparellings of a fishing craft were seen tossing in the waves ; but if any misgivings still remained as to the fate of the boat, they were cruelly put to rest, and for ever, within the week, by the spars which were cast ashore on the sea board of Dunbar, and recognised as those of the "John and Mary." The sufferers who thus perished in the full bloom of life, with their widows and orphans, are as follows :—John Smith, master and owner of the boat, aged thirty, left a widow and four children, the eldest five years, the youngest eleven months ; James Fleming, over forty, left a widow pregnant, besides seven children from two to sixteen years old ; Henry Reid, forty-five, left a widow and seven children, five of whom were under fourteen years, the youngest being born the same morning on which the father perished ; Thomas Fleming, bordering on fifty, left a widow and six children, four of whom were from nine to sixteen years old, but his son John, a fine young man about twenty, now shared his fate ; James Dick, twenty-three years old, left a widow and two children, eldest five years ; David Birrell, perhaps the most powerful and resolute man in Cellardyke, left a widow

pregnant ; James Dickson, unmarried, aged twenty-seven.
He was the solitary survivor in the loss of the " Lord Melbourne ;" and thus, in little more than seven years, no fewer
than thirty brave men of Cellardyke perished at sea.

> " Far down below the sounding wave,
>   Still shall they lie though tempests o'er them sweep ;
> Never may flower be strewn above their grave—
>   Never may sister weep."

On that memorable morning the fleet, instead of tacking for
" Skimfie," bore up for " Stinkin' Hin," as the old fishers
called Anstruther harbour, which became almost from that
day, for the sake of its unrivalled fairway and cosy lee, the
constant rendezvous of the Cellardyke boats ; nor let us forget
that these had for a second time outgrown the accommodation
of their own little harbour. The fishermen, as we saw, in
virtue of the old charter between the two lairds, had a free and
unchallengeable right to Anstruther harbour—a right which
was now more valued, because more to the general interest,
than any other in the common good, whether of burgh or
barony. It left, of course, the vicarage teinds in the original
position, these being still leased from the superior by a committee acting for the community, at an annual rent of £40 or
£50.

CHAPTER XIV.

THE RAILWAY AND THE FISHERY.

Glancing back over the last thirty years, let us here briefly notice the extraordinary changes which have taken place in the condition and prospects of the Fife fisheries.

The railway and the steamer are now scattering in their royal progress the fruits of sea and shore. Turning to the cod and ling fishery in the middle of last century, we see the cream of the sea in the hands of the Falls of Dunbar, at less than 7s a score. Fifty years after their bankruptcy, the trade was so active that the cure at Anstruther alone is estimated by the assistant minister —the Rev. David Wallace—writing in 1837, at six hundred barrels a year. The price, however, did not advance, nor indeed was it always sustained till 1841, when no little excitement was caused in Cellardyke by a new merchant offering a shade less than 12s a score for the season, which, by immemorial usage, ran from the first of winter till the closing week of Lent ; but in these days, when the railway brings within the morrow the sea harvests at Anstruther pier, on the dinner table in London or Manchester, we almost hear the impatient order of the lady or mistress of the house in the impulsive bidding and " the unheard o' prices," as the ancient curer said, with a wicked bite at his tobacco " chew," of our own " representatives " from the leading fish firms in England, now drawing their supplies direct from the East of Fife.

The crab and lobster fishery is another no less eloquent testimony. A century ago the London merchant saw that he was on the right side of the ledger, when he hired the " Well Smack " to

G

run as a lobster trader to the Scottish shore, where they were
fished at a few scattered points, such as Cellardyke and Crail,
at the rate of 5s a score.   But the first whistle of the
railway train across the Border gave such an impetus to the
demand as to double the price within the year.   " They'll be
a shillin' the piece yet," said the old Bailie, referring to a
time when they were not worth the landing, and the predic-
tion has been more than realised.   There was no such intro-
duction, however, to the crab or partan fishing, which the
honest Ceres crofter, who acted as a kind of pioneer to the
trade, not inaptly described " as jist a railway bairn."   Every
grizzled beard, indeed, had seen them fished, if fished at all,
for handline or haddock bait ; and more, he would tell you in
his own Fife way, " was driving saut to Dysart," because any
day, especially after the weird " three fills o' May flood,"
they were to be gathered in bushels amongst the low water
rocks, no one thinking them worth king's coin, unless,
perhaps, when a " twalpenny " or two was given to a needy
neighbour for saving you trouble about a little parcel for the
cousin's children in the country, or an old friend in the city,
who still retained the schoolboy liking for " wilks and partan
taes."   Old John Robertson, of the herring kiln, tried to
storm the Dundee palate with crabs so far preserved by the
boiling process, but in the end he had to confess " they didna
pay kindling for the big pat."   The same expedient was
occasionally acted upon by others ; but till the iron horse was
put into harness the partan was of so little value that a
" dizen o' big taes for a penny " was an everyday errand in
the season to the fisher's door.   Now, however, a new industry
has been added to the coast, and with the miners and cotton
spinners of Lancashire, not to speak of Billingsgate amongst
the customers, the price of this once despised shell fish has

become fourfold in less than twenty years. Indeed, every turn of the tide, every cast of hook or line, is more or less a debtor to the railway ; but it is never so true as of the winter drave, which you will remember in connection with the lively anecdote of the "Box Harry," or Bailie Darsie and the herrings. It is of all others the harvest on the fallow ground, springing up with a new and richer sheaf after the steam plough. " They'll no dae," mutters the little fishcurer, as he crumples up the advices of the last consignment of bloaters, ruined by the foul winds, encountered by the London smack, or her rival, the lumbering old paddle wheel steamer. But another and widely different field is for a time the hope of the Fife trader, till a visit to the bookseller's shop in Anstruther one day undeceives you. " It'll ruin us and our herrin' market," cried the old Bailie, scarlet with rage over the proposed emancipation of the slave in the West Indies, to which large consignments had been sent towards the diet of the negroes ; but in spite of pickled herrings and more powerful interests, abolition came, when the curers had once more to look about for a new customer. An outlet was at last found in sending out the catch almost wholesale as red herrings, a description of article usually and not inaptly referred to as " wissened sticks." A shilling a hundred was reckoned a fair price in those days, but a change was at hand, though no one might see or suspect it—that February morning, in the year 1849, as the muffled up old English skipper went rocking like a cock-boat down the pier as the herring boats began to creep in one by one through the haze. Forty winters in the North Sea had left the old sailor as bashful as a school girl, and this, with his asthma, made him unfit to be his own buyer ; but an electric tailor from the uplands of Ceres was at his elbow, and that morning his orders cost less than half the money they must have done at

Newhaven. " I owe the secret to a torn letter, just as much and no more left to tempt me down," said Skipper Mooltan, chuckling over his discovery, which, however, was blown within the week, when another class of traders appeared upon the scene. Now it was youth and energy, as in the case of Thomas Brown, of Lowestoft, and others, backed not with letters of credit but with bagfuls of new sovereigns and commissions from the best fish stalls in England. There was a long link then needed between the East of Fife and the great artery, but the steam towing service of Leith was hired to the last boat, till a dozen or so have churned away from Anstruther pier with " straw taps " for the Edinburgh railway station. " They're the life o' the shore they English chaps," said the herring skipper. " It's the ass's gallop wi' them," sneered the evil prophet already referred to. But it was not. The next season and the next saw them returning with larger commissions and in greater force, and even the loungers with their hands buried deep in their pockets at the "Wheengin' Brig," confessed that "the old book had got anither leaf and was the better for't." The river was rising ; the old eddies throbbed with the new life, the waifs and straws danced to the generous music. It was no passing wave, but the stream swelling on the dry sands, and wafting in the harvest, which from that day lent a new and kindlier destiny to sea and shore.

There was once an old fisher of Cellardyke who cast a knot as another would make an entry in the log-book concerning the disasters of the sea, and now the thread would run unbroken through the horny fingers for his reckoning of seven years or less when the fatal mark again told like a whisper the sad old story. Then, as you remember, the black clouds of winter curtained the mariner's grave ; but now the golden harvest gladdened the sunny shore, when the exulting cry, " the herrin's in the Haiks," sent the boats like bees in rosy June to the ancient rendezvous. It was Monday, the 20th of August 1855, and for once the hopes of the coast were more than realised. That season Cellardyke had so far outgrown any former fleet as to have over a hundred and thirty boats at the Lammas drave. The herring shoal also has never been exceeded, and boat after boat was laden to the gunwale, amongst others being the "Venus," which had a haul of nearly eighty barrels. With a calm sea there was no danger, but unfortunately the west wind freshened into a gale, when the old craft, in the gathering twilight, was seen to make sail for home. "My dead mother beckoned to me last night," said one of the crew, and the presentiment was sadly fulfilled, for in the offing of Crail the overburthened boat was struck first by one and then by another roaring billow, which utterly overwhelmed her. There was a chance for life, however. She did not sink, and the crew clung to the wreck, these being Adam Reid, the skipper and owner of the boat, and his two sons, Adam and William, the latter a boy about eight years of age; and three half-dealsmen, Kenneth M'Leod, from the Isle of Skye; James Malcolm, Dundee; and David Laing, Arncroach. And so they struggled in the darkness and the tempest, with every wave breaking over them as they hung on the dismantled wreck. The youth had found a heroic guardian in his elder brother, but within the hour his old father and Kenneth, the Islesman, were martyrs to the storm. The others, faint and exhausted, were clinging with the grasp of despair, when two hours later their cries attracted the notice of the St Monance boat in charge of William Mathers, who bore down to their rescue. Touching to tell poor Malcolm perished with the relief cheer ringing on the waters, and the youth, like a smitten blossom, was lifeless in his brother's arms, when he and David Laing were dragged through the surf by the life lines on board the friendly boat, which at once hastened, with all the speed that a contrary wind would admit, to Anstruther. Four perished and two survived, the corpse of the little brother being brought ashore with them ; and one of the most touching sights ever seen on the streets of Cellardyke, was that morning when the desolate widow— with a grief on her face too deep for sighs or tears—bore home her darling as if hushed not in death, but in the nestling sleep of a mother's bosom.

The next boat disaster, which was painfully akin to the sinking of the " Lord Melbourne," occurred on Friday, the 8th December 1859 ; but here let us observe that other tragic incidents had more than once cast a shadow on the shore. Thus about thirty years before a fine young man, Andrew Robertson, fell overboard and was drowned in a boat race towards a large ship, which was flying her colours for a pilot in the offing of Cellardyke. Again in 1835 an intrepid fisherman, Thomas Birrell, lost his life in the act of trimming the sail. He made an heroic struggle for life, and had so far succeeded that he was hand in hand with one of his boat mates ; but his sea glove slipped, and he fell backward to a watery grave. Thomas Birrell belongs on the mother's side to the old sea captains of Anstruther, that shared as few have shared in the romance of the deep. Many sleep in a sailor's grave, and this, like his own, was also the fate of his brother, the loss of whose boat it is now our melancholy province to tell. She was the " Heroine," an Anstruther built clipper, which had sailed that morning to ply the haddock or small line fishing near the Marr or inner reef. At that time the crew carried eight " ties " or " hundred " of line to a hand,

and having worked her fishing gear the " Heroine," with the
sea studded all round with the wing-like sails of the fisher
boat, bore away for the land. The south wind was blowing
so strong that the foresail was fully half-reefed as the boats
came flying, like the sea birds, through the driving mist.
The waves were also tossing wild and high, and a brave hand
was needed to "luff," or " keep away " to wind and sea, till at
last danger seemed left behind in the kindly Forth. So it
was on board of the " Heroine," as three of the crew, like men
after an harassing watch, were seen, bread kit in hand, to enter
the cabin, which they had scarcely done when a great wave,
swift and terrible as the chariot of death, rolling in from the sea,
dealt the fatal stroke, which sent the ill-fated boat to the
bottom. A consort boat, the " Union," Skipper George
Barclay, was perhaps not two hundred yards to leeward, and
not an instant was lost in tacking to the rescue ; but so quick
and ruthless had been the work of the destroyer that one man
alone clung to a floating plank. He caught the friendly line,
and was taken on board the " Union," which, as it was in vain
to tarry on the scene of death, at once hoisted all possible
sail for Anstruther to land the survivor, and break the melancholy tidings of the loss of the boat and seven of the crew.
The disaster occurred at noonday, and was so near as to be
witnessed from the Fife shore as well as from several of the
boats, which crowded, though all too late, to the fatal scene,
where, strange as it may appear, the sea was now so calm as to
be really like a refuge place in the storm. The survivor was
Daniel Fleming. The seven sufferers were—Wm. Birrell, skipper
and owner, aged forty-three, whose household consisted of his
wife and four sons, the oldest, David, aged seventeen, as well
as his nephew, Thomas Birrell, sharing his fate ; James Davidson, another nephew, left a widow and two little daughters ;

William Wood, known far and near as the precentor in the
Parish Church, left a widow and nine children ; George Kay,
left a widow and three children ; James Reid, but a few months
married, left a widow, who became a mother long after his
gallant father lay entombed in the waves.   The day following
the calamity was one of tempest and storm ; but on Sabbath
a squadron of some fifteen or sixteen boats went out to search
for the bodies.   Hook and line were cast and recast over the
place where the boat was seen to founder ; but the volunteers
returned from the pious errand without finding either the
wreck or the hapless crew.

> " Alas ! the pillows
>   Of that uneasy bed
> Rise and fall with the billows
> O'er our sailors' head."

The 10th of May 1865 was another grief-stirring day in
Cellardyke.   The month opened in witching loveliness.   The
birds sang, the leaves and the blossoms danced in the sunny
air.   The beauty of spring was on land and sea, and the fisherman, like the farmer, was at work with a diligent hand, not
in sowing, indeed, but in gathering the generous spoils of the
main.   Most of the boats had taken to the haddock lines ; but
several, including the " Helen," one of the largest and finest
of her class, of which Henry Beat was skipper and owner,
continued at the ling and cod fishery.   The voyage promised
well, so well, indeed, that the little squadron had been betrayed
to an unusual distance in the North Sea, where they were
overtaken by a dreadful gale from the east-north-east.   Night
blackened in with the storm on sea and sky ; like the sea birds
overhead every gallant boat was now hastening to the shore.
It became as dark as the grave.   The eye was baffled and lost,
except, perchance, when the breakers would flit like ghosts

amongst the gathering shadows. " I never was at sea in a
nicht like this, men," said a grey-haired fisher, and every hour
seemed to increase the perils of the voyage, especially when
crossing the dangerous reefs, where the broken seas were as
treacherous to the keel as drifting sand or snow to the foot of
the wanderer astray in the midnight storm ; but in the
language of the heroic skipper, who rubbed the salt out of his
eyes next morning on Anstruther pier, " God was the pilot,"
and boat followed boat to the friendly shore. The tread of the
big boots echo through the streets, and loving households wait
and watch, expecting the next comer to be their own. The fire
is trimmed ; the table is set ; mother and children are looking
out at window and door ; but one crew tarries longer than the
rest. It is the " Helen," and all day long eyes are straining
to catch the well-known sail ; but night comes, and then the
morrow, and then the night again, but still no tidings from
the weary sea. At last—alas ! how slowly and how reluctantly
—the telescope is shut, and the door is closed, and friends go
out and in, their eyes red with weeping, in the home of the
widow and the orphan. The " Helen," like the other deep sea
going boats of the time, had eight of a crew, the sufferers
being—Henry Beat, skipper, left a widow and four children ;
Thomas Brown, a widow and two children ; Thomas Reid, like
the former, a brother-in-law of Skipper Beat ; Andrew Robertson, a wife and seven children ; Thomas Wood, a wife and
three children ; Daniel Fleming, a wife and two children ;
Francis Montidore and Thomas Muir, both unmarried. The
widow and the orphan, however, were not forgotten ; for by the
middle of July over three hundred and eighty pounds had been
subscribed as a relief fund, chiefly through the exertions of Mr
David Murray, of St Ayles. The outgush of sympathy was
far and near ; but in the universal feeling of the hour one aged

mother, whose heart was wrung with no common anguish, was especially remembered, and well may it have been so, as her life story will tell. It is as follows:—" Mrs Reid, one of the most remarkable women ever connected with the Scottish shore, died in Cellardyke on Saturday, the 25th February 1873, in the sixty-ninth year of her age. There is many a mournful tale of the sea—' the cruel and remorseless sea '—but few have had so much cause to lament over the weary waters as the aged pilgrim who then entered into her rest. Mrs Reid, or Agnes Birrell, to give her maiden name, belongs to one of the most numerous families of Cellardyke of our day ; but her father, a strong-limbed, clear-headed, sea-faring native of Kinghorn, was the first of his race in the East Neuk, where he had taken to himself a wife from that fine old stock, the sailor Robertson's of Anstruther. Agnes, as the strapping fisher lass, married her promising townsman, James Davidson, and a happier young couple never crossed the Old Kirk stile of Kilrenny, but the sun was to go down on the very morning of their joy. On the 24th of September 1828, her husband, as one of his father's crew, as was the custom at that time with the Cellar-dyke fishermen, had gone round with the boat to the Eden for mussel bait, and was lying ready to sail in the river, when the wind rose violently from the westward. The older hands wished to remain at their moorings, but the young men were impatient to be again with their wives and sweethearts, and though one of the crew predicted the coming disaster as he stepped on board—' There'll be mussels scauppet the day whaur they never were before '—the sail was hoisted, and the boat dashed out to sea. The little craft reeled gallantly through St Andrews Bay, and tacked to windward of the Carr ; but while crossing the stormy ' Hurst ' she was struck by a dreadful sea. It was the old sad, sad story : the boat

rolled over on the weather side, and lay unbosomed and helpless to the next stroke of the waves, which rushed like a
cataract over the gunwale. ' She is sinking,' and a
long, wild cry rose over the hoarse roar of the storm as the
poor fishermen cast their farewell look on sea and shore ; but
James Davidson and his father, as lovingly and trustingly as
in the old days of childhood, and as if death could never
divide them, clasped each other round the neck, and so sunk
together into a watery grave. His old uncle was saved to tell
the affecting story, which made a deep impression at the time
on the public mind, though it could fall on no ear with the
same heart-crushing misery as on that of the young widow,
who nursed her new born child in the silence of the night,
with the saddest of all music, the wail for the loved and lost.
But time softens every grief, and as years rolled on the widow
became once more the happy wife and joyful mother of five fine
children. Her second husband, Thomas Reid, was an enterprising fisherman ; and his fine new boat, the ' Nancy,' of
Cellardyke, had only been a fortnight at sea when she
foundered during the memorable gale on the night of the 23d
April 1846, about fifteen miles, as it was supposed, from the
Isle of May, when all on board perished, ' with no ear to pity
and no arm to save.' There were seven of a crew, and six
widows and fifteen fatherless children left to mourn their
untimely fate ; but the bereaved widow had not drained the
cup of affliction. Her handsome brother, Thomas, was one
day accidentally drowned at sea. But on the 8th of December
1859 her bleeding heart was again torn by the loss of another
Cellardyke boat, with her gallant brother William, and her
own eldest son—the child of her first love, James Davidson—
who perished like the rest of the crew, with the exception of
one survivor, who was spared to tell with what martyr-like

constancy brave men could meet their fate. Three brothers
of Mrs Reid's second husband had years before met a similar
death ; but the afflicted widow again participated in no
common measure in the last distressing calamity which befel
Cellardyke, when her son Thomas—the Benjamin of her household—and her two sons-in-law suffered with all hands by the
foundering of their boat in the North Sea on the stormy night
of the 10th of May 1865. By these accumulated disasters
Mrs Reid has lost two husbands, two sons, two sons-in-law,
two brothers, and three brothers-in-law ; or to include nephews
and other connections, more than twenty near relations have
perished by the sea; and was it then strange that after all these
manifold afflictions the bereaved wife and mother should love
to linger where she could gaze out on the far away German
Sea—' the weary sea,' as she would say—and listen so wistfully
now in the still summer gloaming, to the voice of the waves
in their soft hymn-like murmurings ; or, again, in the night of
gathering storm, when the billows trampled the shore fierce
and loud as the crash of battle—for both to her was full of
meaning—sadder it could not be, yet falling on the quivering
heart with all the pathos of the dirge song to the mourner
sitting by the lonely grave. But while mourning long and
truly for the dead, she never forgot her duty to the living.
There is no situation in the ordinary lot where woman is more
truly the helpmate of man than as the fisherman's wife, for
she is not only the companion of his home and the mother of
his children, but in all the operations of the busy year, her
industry as her thrift is the secret of his prosperity and
welfare. Mrs Reid was one of these people you never find
idle ; but her nimble fingers were not confined to the common
duties of her sphere, for in her earlier years she handled the
tar and paint brush on her husband's boat with all the skill

of a tradesman, and this energy of character may be said to have remained with her to the last, as only that winter she was to be seen gathering limpets from the rocks as bait for the fishing line. The old heroine was also remarkable for her sterling Scottish independence, and ungrudgingly toiled from sunrise to sundown on a long summer day, in order, as she said, ' never to be obleeged either to frien' or frem ;' and so her life past on with exemplary diligence and usefulness, till she was struck down a few months before by paralysis; but it is pleasing to know that as the evening shadows deepened around her— the heralds of the coming change—her spirit rejoiced in the hope of the better and brighter day, and of reunion with the loved ones ' not lost but gone before.' "

And thus many and sad have been the unspoken farewells, the thrilling sorrows of the sea ; but the direst and most heartrending of all, so far as our narrative leads, is that which is still to be told. We refer to the dreadful sacrifice of black Friday, the 19th of November 1875, when no fewer than five East of Fife boats, with all on board, were lost in the English seas. It was on the homeward voyage from a fishing adventure, which illustrates more than any other the indomitable energy and enterprize of the mariners of Fife. Centuries ago the old fathers fished the herring at the Lewis, and the cod at the Orkney Isles. Seventy years ago and less the fishers of Fife led the Lammas fleets of Wick, as they do to-day, along the Buchan coast, but their story is never so interesting and romantic as in connection with the Norfolk fisheries. About two-and-twenty years before our narrative opens, some four or five Cellardyke boats had as many seasons fished the summer herring from old Yarmouth quay, but scarcely ten seasons had come and gone since the first adventure on the autumn sea. It came about in this way : Profitting by a hint on

Fisherrow beach, the skipper of the old " Hope " sailed to the
southward, but on arriving with his Fifeshire gear he and
his crew were exactly in the sad plight of gold seekers
without a single hammer or pick to break into the mine.
There were those who laughed ; but unmoved and un-
daunted they at once rigged their twenty nets with cork
and messenger, and thus, like their English neighbours,
went to sea, where they in the end prospered so well
that they returned home with £32 to a hand, or in other
words, with a double harvest as compared with hook and line.
This was in 1863, and the following autumn the lucky little
craft and a companion boat renewed the venture, which from
that day so engaged the enterprise of the coast season after
season that we find the departure on the fatal cruise thus related in an Anstruther news-letter :—" After a brief respite
from sea labour, but at the same time after a season of in-
cessant sweat and hurry in the double work of 'drying up' the
old fleet, and preparing for another harvest—our fishermen
are again taking their departure for the romantic coast of
Yarmouth. The pioneer of the fleet, with the same gladsome
north-easter, the welcome 'Lady Anst'er wind,' which was
whistling the choicest of all music through the golden sheaves,
hoisted foresail and mizen, and so with flowing sheet sped
merrily across the sparkling Forth on the distant voyage.
Two Banffshire 'skaffies,' which were waiting in Anstruther
harbour for a convoy, or to speak the truth, 'a pilot through
the deeps,' also headed to sea, and in the course of the morning tide several of the Cellardyke crews were likewise afloat and
speeding southwards like seabirds on the wing, while, need we
say that from many a quiet retreat, moistened eyes gazed long
and lovingly after the fast receding sails. Notwithstanding
the friendly breeze, however, the great bulk of the crews will

not leave till Monday, when, unless the weather is all the worse, the shore will be well nigh as deserted as in Lammas, as Cellardyke is expected to send over forty boats to Yarmouth or the sister station of Lowestoft. An English buyer writes, 'Little doing, and that little far away at sea. Quality also small, and only finds a market, because, like the hungry man, there is no choice in the bill of fare ; but I fancy it is with us here, as it was with my friends at Stonehaven and Aberdeen, There'll be no luck till the Dykers come.'" The subject is thus continued in the following week under the text of a run to Yarmouth :—" In the course of Wednesday the remaining crews hoisted sail, and telegrams have been thus early received announcing the safe arrival, after a fine run of from thirty-two to fifty hours. Several boats had sailed on Thursday week, but these encountering the northeast gale had taken shelter in the creeks of the coast, and only left their moorings to join the squadron, which crossed the harbour bar at Anstruther with Monday's tide. The passage south seems, indeed, to have been a sight to see, as the picturesque sails full to the breeze, ploughed a foaming track through the dark blue waves at a speed which made the magnificent regatta all their own. In more than one instance the voyage was run with a swift trading screw, and as the little fairies sped past the sooty steam colliers of the Tyne, 'Geordie,' with a sailor's candour, had to rattle his compliments, ' She sails like a witch, hinny,' while saucy Montrose men, who usually lead the windbound fleet, gave an extra pull to their lofty royals, but all in vain, being lost to leeward much in the same way as a dashing car leaves behind the labouring wain. We learn that there are nine crews from Pittenweem this season at the south, and about thirty from St Monance — those from Cellardyke being little

short of fifty first-class deep sea going boats." But bad
news, which always travels swiftly according to the proverb,
were soon received of storm and disaster, and on Friday
morning, the 22d of October, it was known in Cellardyke that
a gallant fisher had perished in the gale of the previous night
at Lowestoft. The incident is thus specially referred to in a
news letter of the 30th of the month:—"Letters and telegrams
from the Norfolk Coast this week bring only one tale—namely,
stormy weather and fruitless labour. The boats during the
season have night after night watched like blockade runners
for a passing chance at the fishing ground, but were unable to
venture from behind the great sand banks which, however
fatal to the unwary mariner, yet serve to shield the shore from
the fury of the surge, and men have grown grey in the voca-
tion who do not remember so little work with the net as in the
October of the present year. As at home, a lull in the gale
on Monday allowed the fleet to go to sea, but they were
lucky who saved their drifts, which in many cases were dismantled by the gale. Little or nothing, therefore, has to
be said of the doings of our crews since our last report; but
it is yet hoped that with a favourable change the errand may
still be overtaken before our fishermen steer for the north. At
Lowestoft the melancholy accident to James Gardiner has
caused a dark cloud over the spirits of the East of Fife men.
The crew were one family in kindred or feeling, but poor James
was the guiding spirit, trusted and loved by all, and thus his
post was the tiller on the fatal Thursday night the boat
ventured to sea. Few, indeed, excelled him as a helmsman,
and under his skilful hand the gallant craft sped merrily on
her stormy course till she was rounded to on another tack.
The manœuvre was cleverly done, but seeing his comrades
struggling with the sail as it wildly tossed in the rising gale,

the generous steersman sprang from his seat to give a helping hand, but the heroic act cost him his life, for in stepping forward he was caught by the sail and thrown into the sea. He was never seen again, finding a martyr's grave, as we may say, where many a brave man rests from the battle and the storm. James Gardiner was in his forty-seventh year, and unmarried; but the sister who shared his home, and many friends, will long lament the fate of as gallant and true a heart as ever sailed from the shores of the Forth." His memorial stone in Kilrenny Churchyard is thus inscribed :—

> " A watery grave we do not dread,
> The sea shall render back its dead,
> And restore each scattered bone ;
> And land us safe on Canaan's shore,
> Where sin and death divide no more
> The glorious land of home."

And so the sand trickled down the glass till some three weeks had come and gone, when the crews once more packed up their sea chest and prepared for the homeward run. But again the storm was booming on the lee, and the Sabbath before their departure is thus remembered on the shores of Fife. Thus we read of the Lord's Day of the 14th of November :—" The sea wall at the golden strand of Cellardyke having been beaten down by the fury of the waves during the early tide of Sabbath, and the herring boats wintering on the ground being thus in imminent danger, it was found necessary to call out the inhabitants by the town officer and his bell to lend a helping hand to save them. Such a duty was quite a thing of course with old James Wilson some fifty years ago, but the unwonted summons had a startling effect on the Cellardyke of to-day ; but nevertheless men, women, and children at once hastened to the scene of action. Vener-

H

able elders of the Free Church, sedate deacons also, and exemplary Christians of all denominations, stayed only to exchange church-going coats for less dainty garments, and then hastened with quicker footsteps on the errand of duty. It was no easy task to drag the big boats up the soft bank, in which the busy workers sank ankle deep at every step ; but 'where there's a will there's a way,' says the old proverb, and a right noble illustration it had on this memorable Sabbath morning, for the men had no sooner adjusted roller and lever than the signal 'haul awa',' saw the rope tighten in the grasp of the willing matrons, who, like true heroines, never once rested nor yielded to fatigue till the six or seven boats which were in peril had been placed beyond the reach of the flood. As an instance of the urgency of the situation, we may state that one or more of the boats had been filled with spray, and had to be pierced to drain it off; indeed, the safety of much valuable property was simply due to the spontaneous help of the community without distinction of sex, age, or calling." The tempest, as we gather from an extract, was of almost unparelleled severity. Up to Saturday last the weather for the week was singularly settled for late autumn, a keen frost, especially after nightfall, dispelling the mists which so often obscure a November sky ; but if pleasant on shore it was far otherwise at sea, and vessel after vessel arrived in the Forth confirming the report of heavy gales in the far offing. The wind rose on Saturday, but the surf outran the gale, as usually happens with storms in the North Sea, and night closed as one of the most threatening and dismal ever remembered by old sailors on the shores of Fife. As in the dreadful gale only a month ago the tides were unusually full, and the waves thus hurled with unbridled fury against the sea defences, so wrecked and dismantled, the consequences have been in a melancholy degree disastrous to property, though happily neither life nor limb has suffered on this occasion. Captain Miller, with a half-century's experience, informs us that he never saw so much surf on Anstruther beach ; but with the exception of snapping their mooring chains, no damage was sustained by the craft in the harbour. The storm, however, suddenly subsided; but to resume the narrative, which goes on to tell that, in order to avail themselves of the moonlight for their long and hazardous voyage, a number of the crews this week left Yarmouth for home. A fleet of some twenty-five Scottish boats sailed with the evening tide of Monday, and four of the Cellardyke squadron arrived at Anstruther in the same tide on Wednesday. Many others are on the homeward run, and on the braehead and almost every outlook where the eye can sweep to seaward of St Abbs, little groups were to be seen on the following days watching for the well-known sail which should once more bring " luck " and gladness to the lone fireside. Not a few of the homes by the sea have been cheered in this way ; but a number of the crews have signified their intention to continue for some time longer at the south, owing to the very encouraging success on the Norfolk coast. On Monday evening, some fortunate crews are said to have earned from £50 to £100, thus adding still more to the singular vicissitudes of the season, seeing that while some crews are reported to have grossed from £300 to £500, others will not clear the expenses of the trip. An unfortunate accident happened on Friday week at Yarmouth to the fine Cellardyke boat " Favourite," which took fire during the absence of the crew. The fire was caused by the cabin stove, and was only extinguished by the scuttling of the boat after damage to the hull, tackle, and the clothes of the crew exceeding £100.

" Mind, lassie, and rin for the papers next week. Your faither 'll be at the fireside, an' it'll be so grand to read the welcome hame," exclaimed a devoted mother, glancing over the paragraph ; but, alas ! weary weeks came and went before the bereaved widow could turn to the prised page—and then, alas! not to read of united and joyous homes, but how near and dear ones had suffered and died. Here is the account written in the first burst of grief and despair :—" Dreadful as have been the tempests of the season, none have proved so sad and disastrous as the north-east storm which raged along the coast from Friday morning till Sunday, and which has added one of its blackest chapters to the weary chronicle of the sea. The haddook fishers all along the Scottish seaboard were busily plying hook and line when the gale burst upon them like a thunder peal, scattering the boats in every direction, and threatening to consign one and all to the swoop of the Destroyer as the martyrs of Fate. In many cases the poor mariners were only rescued in the last extremity. One of these hairbreadth escapes was in the case of the Arbroath yawl ' Integrity,' the crew of which were snatched from the brink of the grave by the deep sea going boat of Skipper Archibald Peebles ; but, unfortunately, in the leap for life, one of the perishing men, named Thomas Beattie, was nearly crushed to death between the two boats. Skipper Peebles and his comrades not only did what they could for the comfort of the crew, but they also took the boat in tow and landed her at Pittenweem, where their humane example was seconded by the inhabitants, who opened a subscription, in particular for the relief of poor Beattie, whose injuries included a broken thigh bone. The conduct of the Pittenweem men on this occasion appears to more advantage from its noble con-trast with the cruel indifference of the master of a passing brig,

who left the poor men to perish. The same generous assistance was also given by the master of the schooner 'Lord
Clyde,' who took on board the drowning crew of a yawl
belonging to Castle, near Colisten. The yawl was also taken
in tow, but had to be abandoned off Girdleness by the parting
of the thwart to which the rope was fastened. The crew
were landed on Saturday morning at Elie, and the skipper,
James Philp, and his three neighbours, made their way to St
Monance, where the inhabitants at once saw to their necessities,
and furnished them with the means to return home. But we
only linger on the threshold of the dreadful tale. Old seafolk
describe the storm as the most dreadful in their experience,
whether for the suddenness of the outbreak or the fury with
which it assailed them. The first whistle of the blast, like
the preconcerted signal in war, roused the sea in raging
billows, which, like white-plumed squadrons, everywhere
swept the wide and weary prospect as the messengers of
death. Who shall tell the terror of the fisherman's home
with the hoarse cry of the tempest ringing like a dirge wail
on the shore. Nor were their fears the idle terrors of the
night, for many an eye red with weeping, tender hearts
breaking with despair, will never, oh! never, again be
gladdened in the shadows of time as in the happy days of the
past.

> ' But thou, my friend, my brother,
>   Thou'rt speeding to the shore
> Where the dirge-like tone of parting words
>   Shall smite the soul no more.
> And thou wilt see our holy dead,
>   The lost on earth and main,
> Into the sheaf of kindred hearts
>   Thou wilt be bound again.'

In the East of Fife the safety of the white fishing boats was soon ascertained ; but it was far otherwise with the large squadron on the long and perilous voyage from the herring rendezvous. Over forty of these boats were caught in the hurricane, some scarcely out of sight of the Norfolk shore, but others almost as nigh the dear old headland of St Abb's on the other side of the Forth. The skipper of one of the leading boats gives us the following log leaf :—' We sailed from Lowestoft about noon on Wednesday, and crossed the Deeps with a spanking breeze from the westward. Easy weather off Flamborough Head, but stood to the northward under flowing sheet till to windward of the Ferne Isles, when the warning, which could for some time be read in the driving showers and troubled sky, was followed by the sudden shifting of the wind from the north-west to the north-east, and with scarcely an interval we were in the teeth of the most terrific hurricane I ever encountered at sea.' Several of the homeward bound Cellardyke boats met the Eyemouth crews working their haddock gear, and these, after a long and weary conflict with the wind and waves, reached Anstruther harbour by midnight. Such was the fury of the tempest that the crests were torn from the waves and scattered like snowdrift ; while, unable to hoist sail, the boats were again and again swept by the mountain billows, which but for the protection of the decks must have engulphed one and all in hopeless destruction. The boat in particular of Skipper Alexander Watson split her foresail in rounding St Abb's, and was for a time in great peril on the leeshore of Dunbar. Five boats, as the last chance of safety, ran for shelter into Holy Island, and, though not without risk, ultimately gained safe anchorago. Others obtained a harbour of refuge in Shields and other ports on the coast, but the rear of the fleet bore up for the Norfolk coast as the first hope of shelter. Two lamentable disasters occurred to the leeward part of the Cellardyke fleet. The crew of the boat of Skipper David Wood were tacking for Grimsby after nightfall on Friday, when Alexander M'Ruvie, a promising youth, aged 17, lost his hold and fell into the sea. His father was on board; but how frail is man before the hurricane, and the brave lad sank before his eyes into a watery grave. In Skipper George Anderson's boat his brother-in-law, John Watson, a free-hearted and gallant mariner, 32 years of age, was washed overboard while on duty at the mizen. His comrades did all and more, but it was the old sad, sad story—perchance a pale face, seen for an instant in the dark abyss, a single cry heard, but scarcely heard in the crash of the storm, and so the voyage of life for ever ended. A fearful accident also happened in the Deeps to one of Skipper Robert Davidson's crew. His brother-in-law, Robert Brown, while at the post of danger, was struck in the forehead by the yardarm and rendered insensible. The accident occurred on Saturday morning, but it was not till the boat reached Anstruther harbour on Monday afternoon that medical assistance could be obtained for the unfortunate fisherman, who all the while continued unconscious. On examination his skull was found to be fractured, and grave fears were felt for his recovery. Robert Brown is a married man with a family.

"These were sad calamities, and the report caused a profound sensation on the coast; but they were only the heralds of wider and more thrilling disasters. As night fell on Friday, some six or eight of the boats in the neighbourhood of the Fernes, as an expedient to outbrave the storm, cast from seven to eighteen of their nets, or, it might be with the same object, threw out their big sail, to which they rode as under the lee of a floating breakwater. One of these boats was that of Skipper John Wood, who cut away his drift of fourteen nets, and made sail with the first lull in the storm. The other was the boat of Skipper James Murray, which was at one time within hail, and also for hours in convoy on the Northumberland coast. His boat likewise made every precaution for the night, and one of Skipper Wood's crew saw her light bright as a beacon fire, tossing in the darkness of the storm so late as 9 P.M. The one boat arrived at Anstruther on Sabbath night, but a fatal mystery hangs over the fate of the other and her hapless crew. The same cruel destiny befell another Cellardyke boat—that of Skipper Robert Stewart, who sailed from Lowestoft only about four o'clock on the fatal morning, and who would thus encounter the tempest in all its fury in the waste of waters known as the Deeps. The melancholy waves hold the secret, but the sad story is so far revealed by the fate of the St Monance boat, ' Quest,' which sailed at the same hour from the Suffolk coast, but which, according to a telegram received at St Monance early on Wednesday, had been cast ashore a broken and dismantled wreck on the sands of Norfolk. The two missing Cellardyke boats, ' Janet Anderson,' No. 1176, and the ' Vigilant,' No. 1214, were almost new—the latter indeed only launched for the Lammas fishing. The crew of the ' Janet Anderson ' were—James Murray, skipper, aged twenty-six, who was to have been married on his return home ; Andrew Stewart, aged thirty-four, married, four children—an infant being only born on the Monday after his loss ; William Bridges, aged twenty-two, married, one child ; James Walker, a native of Kingsbarns, married, four children ; Alexander Lothian, a veteran fisher of fifty-four, who had braved many a storm on the Scottish shore, married, four children ; Hugh M'Kay and William M'Kay, two fine young men, cousins, and unmarried, from Portskerrie, in the north of Scotland. Seven men, four wives, and thirteen children. The crew of the 'Vigilant' were—Robert Stewart, skipper and owner, aged forty-two, married, four children ; William Stewart, aged forty-six, married, one child—his wife being also in an advanced state of pregnancy ; James M'Ruvie, aged forty-five, married, three children, in addition to his son James, aged sixteen, who perished with him ; Alexander Doig, aged thirty-two, married, six children—the oldest being scarcely twelve years of age ; Leslie Brown, aged nineteen, unmarried—being six men, four wives, and fourteen children. The crew of the 'Quest' of St Monance, No. 221, were—David Allan, skipper, married, six children ; Robert Allan, his son, unmarried ; William Allan, his brother, married, five children ; Alexander Irvine, married, seven children ; Alexander Hutt, unmarried ; Alexander Latto, unmarried ; David Easson, unmarried ; being seven men, three wives, and eighteen children.

" Words can never tell the heartache and the agony in the homes of Cellardyke and St Monance. Every face is clouded with sorrow, and everywhere you hear the wail of the mothers and children weeping in their bereavement and despair. The first death knell may be said to have sounded with the mournful tidings on Saturday of the fate of young Alexander M'Ruvie, followed on Monday morning by the same sad message of John Watson, the last stay of a widowed mother ; but the friends of the missing crews had to wait on from day to day in cruel suspense, as those who realise the bitter, bitter truth that 'Hope deferred maketh the heart sick.' Under any circumstances the loss of so many brave men, the flower of the Scottish shore, the stay and breadwinners of so many helpless children must be an overwhelming and irreparable calamity ; but there is much, very much, about this unexampled disaster that moistens the cheek with the generous tear. 'For home and children' is ever and may well be the watchword of the hardy mariner toiling and struggling on the midnight sea, far away on a stormy shore ; but now the old streets by the beautiful Forth were once more busy, as crew after crew returned to their own. Then came the kind and cheerful talk of those still on the sea, and fond eyes watched long and lovingly, or ran to welcome every coming sail. The fire burned bright in the hearth, and the children—the little children, who already divided the gifts which a father or a brother was sure to bring, and over which little tongues had been so busy—flew to meet every footstep on the stair. ' He will come next,' the mother would say, and the little household, if disappointed for a moment, would rejoice again. In such a scene, oh ! how slow but how crushing would the sickening thought—the terrible truth—at last steal on the heart. Who, indeed, can fathom the agony of those that

> ' —— Doubt, and fear, and wish and grieve,
>   Believe and long to unbelieve,
>   But never cease to ache ;
>   Still doomed in sad suspense to bear
>   The hope that keeps alive despair ?'

Although dark uncertainty may rest upon the closing struggle, it is only too probable that the boats foundered, going down with all hands in the crash of the storm. ' We could do nothing—we had lost all hope ; but God guided us through,' a brave veteran said to us, with a tear in his eye ; and under that black midnight sky, with the thunder of the storm ringing in the ear, and the foaming breakers on every side, well might the storm-tossed mariners thank God for their deliverance. Amongst the many miraculous escapes was that of the boat of Skipper James Stevenson, who sailed on the morning of the gale, and who was thus overtaken in the Deeps. The most painful anxiety was felt for the safety of the crew; but on Tuesday the gladdening message arrived that boat and men were safe at Lynn. Skipper John Birrell and his crew also came through dreadful sufferings, but happily succeeded in the effort to return to Yarmouth. The boat drove twelve hours before the hurricane, and a large schooner was seen to founder and go down with all hands. But this was only one of many instances where

> ' Backward on her course she drifted,
>   Heeding not her helm ;
> Now on giant waves uplifted,
>   Threat'ning to o'erwhelm.
>   Now adown a vale
> Of dark, angry waters driven ;
> While, like spirits chased from Heaven,
>   Loud the wild wind's wail.'

We turn from this doleful chronicle to notice the generous hospitality shown by the fishermen of Holy Island to the five Cellardyke boats in the Kirkcaldy (K.Y.) register. ' No. 838, John Stewart, skipper; No. 992, Robert Stewart; No. 921, John Boyter; No. 987, Michael Doig; No. 144, Alexander Smith.' The drenched and weary crews were assisted to a safe anchorage, and then conducted to a place of shelter, where they had the comfort of fire and bed—indeed, everything was done that one brother could do for another."

A postscript to the same letter goes on to say:—"St Monance has fearfully shared in this awful visitation, as, in addition to the ' Quest,' other two boats have perished on the sandbanks of the Wash. These are the ' Beautiful Star ' and the ' Thane '—the crew of the former being : James Paterson, the skipper, married, and five children; Robert Paterson, his son, unmarried; William Paterson, married, and six children ; Robert Paterson, his son, unmarried ; David Allan, married, and five children ;

James Allan, unmarried ; David Davidson, unmarried. The crew of the ' Thane ' were—Thomas Fyall, the skipper, married, and two children ; David Laurie, married, and five children ; Lawrence Fyall, unmarried ; Thomas Laurie, married ; Thomas Fyall, married, and one child ; Andrew Allan, unmarried ; Alexander Duncan, married, and two children. Seven men were in each boat, eight of these fourteen being married, with twenty-six children."

Another relict of the " Quest " has been cast up at Stiffkey on the Norfolk coast, where the bag marked " City of Seringapotam " has been identified as belonging to Alexander Latto. An impression was abroad in Cellardyke that the body washed ashore near Cockburnspath, near St Abbs, reported as that of a tall, dark-haired man, having the letters J. M. on the arm, and J. A., with the figure 2, on the fragment of clothing, is that of the skipper of the " Janet Anderson ;" but in crossing the Forth his brother found the rumour to be untrue—the remains being those of some luckless sailor drowned not days but weeks before.

The Cellardyke boat " Waverley," Skipper William Watson, arrived on Wednesday from Burnmouth, where she had taken refuge with the eleven deep sea going boats of the village on Friday evening. Being strangers to the critical harbour, the boat was in great danger, and was indeed only saved by the intrepid humanity of the fishermen, who assisted with the necessary anchors and ropes, and then in the same generous spirit supplied the worn and weary crew with warm food, clothing, and beds, never slackening in their brotherly treatment till the boat was once more under sail for Cellardyke.

This is the most terrible disaster that has ever befallen the fishing towns of Fifeshire, Cellardyke having lost fifteen men, St Monance twenty-one, who leave together eighteen widows and seventy-one fatherless children. Public feeling everywhere responds to this awful dispensation of Providence, and it only remains for us to add that the various ministers of the neighbourhood were unremitting in their endeavours to administer the consolations and promises of religion to the bereaved mourners.

Such was the narrative of the week ; but the grief and excitement did not end here, for day by day, or rather week by week, new and thrilling episodes were added to the dismal tale. The mystery as to the fate of the two Cellardyke boats was soon so far unveiled. Eight days had not elapsed when the scattered fragments of a fishing boat were washed ashore at Cullercoats, a fishing village off Northumberland, and amongst other waifs was a helm, recognised as belonging to the missing boat " Janet Anderson," which, in the opinion of fishing circles, had foundered, if, indeed she had not been sunk by the passing steamer about the time when her light was last seen by the consort crew, who shared the perils of that dreadful night. Saturday, the 10th of December, brought tidings of her ill-fated sister the " Vigilant." This boat was one of the four which hoisted sail about 3 A.M. on the fatal Friday. She was last seen in the delusive interval before the storm under a press of sail. Then came the storm and the wrestle of brave men for life, with the closing scene which had been here on that deadly shoal, the inner Dowsing, some thirteen miles to leeward of the course usually taken when crossing the Deeps. The " Vigilant " was found lying in six fathoms by the Trinity cruiser, while in search of floating or sunken wrecks. A masthead was first seen rising on the melancholy waste, and as it was the cruiser's duty to remove such dangers from the path of vessels, this was accordingly done, when it proved to be the mast of a

Scottish fishing boat, which, by the hot iron marks, and also by the initials on the tackle brought up to the surface, was identified as those of the ill-fated boat. These boats, like the " Quest," foundered and went down with all hands. The struggle was thus short and decisive; but it was otherwise, as we shall see, with the martyrs of St Monance, whose fate was that of the castaway clinging all night in hope to the raft, but perishing in the end with "none to pity—none to hear the last farewell." The grave, where all is hushed, holds the secret, but how fearfully suggestive are the revelations that are to follow: —The steam packet, "Sea Nymph," was on her usual run from Hull to Lynn about eight days after the storm, when the watch observed a floating wreck towards the Lincoln coast. It was a mournful symbol of the cruel sea. The waves were washing over the gunwale of the fishing boat, as she proved to be. There was not a trace of the crew. " Poor fellows, they have been all drowned," said one of the passengers, a sailor's bride, as she wiped the trickling tear, and with this impression shared by all the wreck was taken in tow, and eventually berthed at Lynn. The chances of salvage sent the men of the " Sea Nymph " quickly to work to bale their prize, now seen to be the " Beautiful Star." An entrance was made into the bunk or cabin, in the bow of the boat. Here a terrible discovery was made. Truly it was the chamber of death—five of the crew lying lifeless on the floor. Four friends arrived two days later from St Monance and recognised the bodies, when the two missing men of the crew were ascertained to be the master's son, Robert Paterson, and his young companion, James Allan. All is conjecture, but the fact that Skipper James Paterson was severely cleft in the temple has induced many to believe that the others were giving the assistance or relief they could when their own fate was sealed by the swamping of the boat. But to the end they were faithful to duty. The sail yet attached had been thrown into the sea, as we saw on the Northumberland coast, as the last forlorn hope amongst the breakers, when they had shut the door to wait and die. Who does not turn his thoughts to the fearful scene in that floating grave? A brave veteran once told us of the solemn emotions of such a time. He was sitting alone in the cabin preparing a torch as the signal for life or death, when the boat reeled and fell before a tremendous wave. " It's God's will, and I will die here," was the thought of the awful moment, as he collected himself for the last prayer for mercy, less for himself than for the near and dear ones he would never see again. Nor will that heroic skipper of St Monance be forgotten who, in the last struggle with the breakers on Elie shore, was heard singing as one who sings a bridal song—

> " Here let me wait with patience,
>   Wait till the night is o'er,
>   Wait till I see the morning
>   Break on the golden shore."

And so the singer and the song sank together. " It has been a great harvest time for Christ," writes one, whose praise is in the churches, of the awakenings on the Fife coast, and those who knew James Paterson and his companions, who perished on the Lincoln banks, can believe that the gathering shadows but gave a more exulting note to the hymn of victory which they sang together—spirit rejoicing with spirit—till the scene, but not the song, changed, where night and the storm shall rage no more. The stroke which had disabled the master had also perhaps crushed in the aperture in the cabin roof, though otherwise the boat was all but unscathed. The fishing gear was also lying as it had been stowed away in the hold, and the money of the crew, with many a little keepsake—the touching memorials of home—were collected in the cabin. The fearful discovery at the quayside filled the old seaport of Lynn with the wildest excitement. Public sympathy was everywhere aroused ; the seafaring inhabitants in particular gave way to a general burst of tenderness and pity. Three of the Fife fishers had been Good Templars, and no sooner was this known than the Lynn Lodges, as soon as the inquest had been concluded, undertook the pious duty of consigning the dead to the grave. The funeral took place on Tuesday, when some two hundred and fifty fishermen took part in the procession, which, swelled with the Good Templars and the noble-hearted people of Lynn, would number several thousands. The bodies were conveyed in five hearses from the inn in which they had been first deposited to the beautiful cemetery, where, after an impressive celebration of the funeral service according to the ritual of the Order, they were interred in the section set apart for the burial of the Presbyterian dead, some thousand voices joining in the favourite hymn, " Safe in the arms of Jesus." But the crew of the " Beautiful Star " were not alone. The same terrible tragedy had been enacted on board of her consort the " Thane," which was stranded in the course of the following week on one of the half tide scalps near Boston Deeps. She was lying keel up, with the port gunwale buried in the sand. The " Thane " had at one time been in collision, and eight planks were cut down abaft the main thwart as if by a vessel's stem : but the most alarming discovery made by the dredgers was the bodies of three of the crew stretched in the forecastle. Being unable, in the situation, to remove the ghastly freight, they waited till the succeeding ebb, when the bodies were re-moved to Lynn. They were those of the young men Thomas

Fyall, Thomas Laurie, and Alexander Duncan, the four others, including Skipper Fyall, having in all probability been washed overboard. Though distinguished by no set programme, the funeral of the three men of the " Thane " caused a yet more profound sensation, as the whole population of the seaport rose, we may say, to pay the last tribute of sympathy to the brave mariners who had fallen a sacrifice to this unexampled tragedy. The solemn scene stands alone on the records of Lynn, as the living tide of some nine thousand mourners moved along the road on Sabbath afternoon with their melancholy burthen to the burial yard, where, as grave after grave was closed over the sleepers, the solemn silence was broken by many a sob—men and women, indeed, giving way to unrestrained tears. Three of the relatives were present from St Monance. Such are the untold sufferings of the fatal cruise ; but there were others of the Fifeshire fleet all but within the verge of destruction. " It's all over," said one of our crew. " All of us thought the same ; but God's own right hand was our shield and stay," observed a storm-beaten survivor at the thanksgiving, and who, after such experiences as the following, will marvel that he did so, or that, as the solemn scene recurred to him, with his hard rough hand he wipes the tear out of his eyes. The "Excelsior," David Wood, master and owner, arrived at Anstruther on Sabbath morning, the fifth December. This crew also sailed for home on the fatal morning of the 19th November, and encountered the storm in full fury, with the Yorkshire coast yet many miles to windward. It was a situation to make the stoutest hearts quail— an open boat, with the shadows of night gathering around them on that naked waste of waters, flying and beaten like chaff on the thrashing floor, by the lash of the tempest. Perchance it was at such a moment that the doomed boats

I

bore away in the wild hope of out-running the gale ; but the crew of the "Excelsior," true to the motto of their gallant craft, resolved to keep the sea. "God is with the brave," said the old Scottish fathers, and so, with all around black as the yawning grave, save when the white-crested waves gleamed faintly in the darkness, while the thunder crash of the storm deafened the ear, and all but appalled the stoutest heart, the crew of the "Excelsior" struggled on, though as men who stand in the last wrestle between death and life. A dreadful catastrophe, however, occurred toward midnight. The boat was wearing round before the breakers, and strong arms held down the wildly tossing sail, when just as a noble lad, Alexander M'Ruvie, who had been sent on an errand to the cabin, sprung all unseen to his post, a terrible gust wrenched the yard and threw it against the mast, crushing as it went the legs of the unfortunate youth in torturing agony. His poor father was on board, but was himself stunned at the moment by a stroke of the sea. Another of the crew was all but a victim to a sailor's fate, but a third boatmate, Thomas Watson, crept aft—what was the human voice in the wild roar of the storm—and explained to the master what had happened at the helm. The needful manœuvre was well and promptly done, but the brave lad's hour had come—he was only relieved from the cruel hold of the spar to be tossed by the sail into the sea, where seen but for a moment, he perished as the master was stretching out his hand to save him. With sadder hearts and scarce hoping for deliverance, the crew battled on till daylight, when a friendly sail piloted them into Grimsby, from which they only sailed again on the following Friday. That same evening, however, the threatening sky filled our mariners with anxious thoughts and with them the intention of once more seeking a harbour of refuge, but here the Polar Star of the heart cheered them on through the gloom and the storm—nor was their endeavours in vain, as after a wintry voyage the gallant boat was safely moored by the old pier of Anstruther.

The "Dolphin," William Moncrieff master, was also one of the little squadron which sailed from Lowestoft in the first watch of the fatal morning. She was standing across the Wash, about two miles to windward of the "Vigilant," when the hand to hand conflict began with the tempest. Happily, though faint and weary, the crew were able to regain Lowestoft, where she lay till the end of the following week, when they once more sailed for the north; but on the Yorkshire coast the north-east gale again burst upon them, and as the last chance of perishing men they ran into Bridlington Bay. A lull in the gale saw the boat once more scudding for home, but erelong they were thankful for refuge in Scarborough, where they remained till a happy chance enabled them to return to Anstruther early on Monday morning, more than three weeks after they had first hoisted sail for the North.

But in no case were the adventures so extraordinary as with the Cellardyke boat, "Brothers," Skipper James Stevenson. This boat had been at the fishing ground on the Wednesday evening, but on returning to Lowestoft the stirring sight of the "Excelsior" and two others leaving for home induced this crew also to take a hurried departure. The wind was fair, and foresail and mizen bore the gallant craft merrily along the Norfolk shore. Rounding Cromer, other well-known sails were seen lying to, but the "Brothers" followed fast in the wake of the three boats already referred to, and so the little squadron shot over the broad bosom of the Wash. That noble sentinel, the light ship, was seen to leeward on the Inner Dowsing bank, when the black sky revealed its fearful secret by a terrific gust from the north-east. Well might one brave man look wistfully in the face of another as the crew saw themselves all alone on that open and stormy sea ; but heart nor hand failed as, with close-reefed sail, the boat stood in on the starboard tack. This course was steered till the breakers, and the lead at six fathoms, warned them from the Yorkshire coast, when the boat was once more headed, though with great difficulty, to sea. The storm was then at its fiercest, and one of the bravest veterans that ever sailed the salt seas thought it his duty to whisper his fears—" Men, I doubt we're wrang," but then also came the remembrance of home and children, and the heroic resolve, " We'll at least *do* to the last," and so every man stood to his post, though wave on wave swept the sorely labouring boat like a rock in the tideway. The Dowsing light was again seen faintly to leeward, but ere it was reached tide and tempest had drifted the boat so near the shoal that she was a second time steered towards the land. And thus the fight went on, less in hope, perhaps, than in the stern resolve which, with brave hearts, takes the place of dark despair, when at last daylight broke on the dreadful scene. Slowly the black clouds rolled away, but it was only, to all appearance, to unveil the inevitable fate of the crew, for driven to leeward of the Humber, where on that strange and stormy shore could they turn for shelter? But help came where it was least to be hoped for. Weary and exhausted with the fearful sufferings of the night, the strength—but not the calm trust on the mercy of God—was well nigh gone with the crew, when, like an angel in response to the prayer of the mariner's home, a sail was seen bearing in from the sea. This was a Grimsby fishing smack running from the gale. Her main-sail was in ribbons ; but this disaster was the salvation of our fishermen, as disabled from tacking for the Humber she was now steering for the Wytham. Who shall tell the joy of the moment as the stranger beckoned the Scottish crew to follow, and so steering in the wake they safely anchored in the river about noon of Saturday; but to give an idea of the extreme perils of the navigation we may state that the consummate experience of the master of the smack unlocked, so to speak, a "swash" or side way accessible only in the crisis, when the storm-swept bar must have been as the gate of destruction and death. Later in the afternoon the boat shifted with another smack to a more secure anchorage under lee of the Lincoln banks, and in the course of Monday she was steered in convoy with two river craft so far up as Clayholes, a little hamlet some five miles from Boston. The hamlet is one of those romantic resting places by the river brink which may be called "The Sailors' Wayside Inn," and here the kind-hearted English matron heard our fishermen's story, and with true womenly sympathy did all that could be done to assist them. She it was who by sending a pony through the fens to Boston transmitted the welcome telegram which brightened all faces on the Fife coast on the Tuesday by the ringing cry, "There's word fae Steenson." Friends, we remember it well, took courage and said, "All's well; the next message will be our own," but Heaven had its own deep mysteries.

Guided by the friendly English fishermen as to the intricate channel of the river, the "Brothers" safely tacked on Thursday to the open waters of the Wash, and the voyage home was once again hopefully begun, but early on Saturday morning another tempest from the north-east drove them into Scarborough. It was ebbing tide, and the signal lights were extinguished, but the boat was steered for the harbour, when, to the dismay of the crew, the "booms" were on the bar. A second time, however, they met with unexpected deliverance in their hour of need, for, in the climax of the danger, a padded ball and line were thrown from the pier into the boat, when, almost in a breath, some two score of strong and willing arms dragged her beyond the reach of the waves. Nor was this all, for at the mere mention of payment the gallant fellows declared with one voice, "Never a penny from a Scottish fisherman." The same generous treatment was given at the Reading Room or Institute. Other boats on the northward voyage also ran into Scarborough, where later in the day the lifeboat was launched to meet any emergency. The weather continued threatening, but anxious to reach home, the "Brothers" made sail from Scarborough on the following Wednesday. They had, however, been little more than ten miles away when the crew were glad to return, and an attempt two days later, when they were twenty miles to the north, was equally unsuccessful; but on Saturday morning the friendly breeze carried them on a prosperous run from the Yorkshire haven to Anstruther, where they arrived on Monday morning, after being twenty-four days on the passage, and after a succession of vicissitude and suffering that have scarcely a parallel in the story of the coast.

We now come to speak of the noble effort made for the relief of the bereaved. The loss of so many brave and useful lives—so many widows and orphans realising, in the first days of mourning, the loss of breadwinner and stay—made, need we say, a profound sensation in the districts, but Christian friends were not indifferent, or careless, or callous to the touching appeal. During the anxious and weary days of the first week, when the fate of the brave men was so far uncertain, Sir Robert and Lady Anstruther evinced the most tender solicitude for their safety, and when hope at last left not a single ray of comfort on the dark and melancholy prospect, he was the first to hasten to the relief of the stricken and helpless families. The hon. baronet is the principal heritor of Abercrombie, and the brave old home of Balcaskie, if not within, is on the immediate border of the parish ; but in the truly Christian mission on which he entered Sir Robert was only following in the footprints of his lamented father, who, as in the similar catastrophe of 1833, was ever first in the cause of benevolence and humanity. But before proceeding further we pause to refer to the touching and unwearied kindness of Lady Anstruther, than whom never sister of mercy did more to soothe and comfort the lonely home, darkened by sorrow and despair. Yes, there are moments in our anguish when the message of the angels is never sweeter than in a sister's tear, when the broken heart has a language all its own, and when, sorely wounded, it must be led, like the bleeding lamb by the wayside, to the feet of Him who only in the day of fear and trouble can say, as on the sea of Galilee, " Peace, be still."

The movement took form in St Monance Town Hall on Saturday, at a meeting of some of the leading parishioners, when, at the suggestion of Sir Robert Anstruther, it was resolved to unite and work in union with a committee in Anstruther to be appointed at a public meeting, and in this way to secure a common fund for the relief of the widows both in St Monance and Cellardyke. An acting committee was chosen, namely, Chief-Magistrate Nicol, Bailies Macfarlan and Robertson, and Messrs James Trainer, merchant ; John Lockie, of the Mission ; George Bridges, boatskipper ; and Thomas Murray, fishcurer.

The landed proprietors of the East of Fife set a noble example, the following contributions having been thus early received for the Relief Fund :—Sir Coutts Lindsay, Bart., of

Balcarres, £50 ; Sir Robert Anstruther, Bart., of Balcaskie, £20 ; Sir John L. Bethune, Bart., of Kilconquhar, £10 ; W. D. Irvine, Esq., of Grangemuir, £20.

In Cellardyke the Rev. Alexander Gregory, the venerable pastor of the Free Church, held a sympathy meeting in Forth Street Hall in the course of Tuesday, when he spoke with singular earnestness and power from the memorable text, " Oh, that they were wise, that they understood this, that they would consider their latter end." At the close Mr Gregory referred to the generous donation of £30 to the Relief Fund by Stephen Williamson, Esq., of Liverpool, who is a native of Cellardyke.

A public meeting was held in the evening in the Town Hall, presided over by Provost Martin. The Rev. Dr Christie, the minister of the parish, made an appeal at some length and with telling effect on behalf of the helpless families, which was appropriately seconded by Mr Oliphant. Mr Alex. Watson, one of the elders of the parish, and others, took part in the addresses, which were the spontaneous utterance of heartfelt sympathy and affection, when it was resolved to divide the town into districts, and to allocate these to a committee to uplift subscriptions. So cordial was the sentiment of the meeting that on a subscription being opened the sum of £68 was entered by those present. At this stage of the proceedings Skipper Thomas Birrell struck an inner chord in every heart by an extempore address, in which he said that he had lost a grand-father, four uncles, a brother, and a son-in-law, not to speak of other relatives, by disasters at sea. Well then could he realise the sorrow of the sorrow-stricken, for he had only to remember his own, and his most earnest sympathies were therefore with the Christian work to which they had now put their hand. The signal of mercy was flying, and he besought the fishermen of Cellardyke to consider that what was the case of the mariners to-day might be the case of their own to-morrow, and he trusted from his heart that one and all would hasten to the help of the widow and the orphan. The hall was crowded, and a cordial vote of thanks brought the interesting meeting to a close.

The committee began their "labour of love" in the morning, and by Thursday the Cellardyke subscriptions exceeded £150, Mr Oliphant, in his own district, having collected £47. The Relief Fund was already over £600, but it is an interesting fact not to be forgotten, as it goes far to answer a reflection sometimes cast on the providence of the fisher home, that of the thirty-seven fishermen lost in the gale, seventeen were members of the Scottish Legal Burial Society, from which their families received about £200. Resuming the movement so well begun in the picturesque old seat of Balcaskie, you find the following appeal, as "a letter to the Editor," under the date of 29th November, sown broadcast through the newspapers over the length and breadth of the land :—

"SIR,—I do not think I need apologise for asking some assistance from the public through your columns for the many amongst the fishing population in our immediate neighbourhood who have suffered from the late storms. We have lost two boats belonging to Cellardyke and three belonging to St Monance, with the whole of their crews ; and the sorrow, misery, and want in those towns are of a kind that I cannot attempt to describe.

"Such a catastrophe, under any circumstances sufficiently dreadful, is in these cases rendered still more calamitous by the fact that many of the boats' crews are closely related to each other by family ties.

"In the town of St Monance, one unfortunate woman, Mrs Paterson, has lost at one blow her husband, her son, two brothers, three nephews, a brother-in-law, and a cousin ; another,

Mrs Allan, about seventy years of age, has lost her two sons, her two nephews, her son-in-law, and two grandsons.

" A public meeting will be convened by the Provost of Anstruther on Monday, the 6th day of December, in order to obtain aid for the sufferers ; and I am authorised to say that subscriptions will be gladly received for them by the Rev. David L. Foggo, the Manse, Abercrombie, St Monance ; Mr Thomas Nicol, Chief Magistrate, St Monance ; the Rev. Dr Christie, the Manse, Kilrenny, Anstruther ; and also by Provost Anderson, Anstruther ; Mr Martin, Provost, Kilrenny ; Mr Tosh, Provost of Pittenweem ; and W. R. Ketchen, Esq., Elie.

"The above two small towns have lost at one blow 37 of the flower of their sea-going men ; 19 women are left widows ; and 72 children are made orphans, besides, several aged persons dependent upon the deceased men have been deprived of their support.—I am, &c.,

" ROBT. ANSTRUTHER."

The public meeting, numerously attended, was held in Anstruther on 6th December, presided over by Provost Anderson, and at which Sir Robert Anstruther, the Rev. Dr Christie, of Kilrenny ; the Rev. Mr Foggo, of Abercrombie ; Rev. Mr Gregory, Anstruther, and others, took part, when a large committee was appointed to collect subscriptions, and a body of trustees was nominated to hold and administer them. In a short time a sum amounting to £7206 15s 3d was raised. Among the more notable contributions may be mentioned one of £100 from Captain Hughes, of Wallaroo ; £50 from Sir Coutts and Lady Lindsay, of Balcarres ; £50 from the Earl of Southesk ; £50 from Charles Gray, Esq. of Nareeb ; £50 from Stephen Williamson, Esq., Liverpool ; £50 from William Baird, Esq., of Elie ; £50 from the Hon. Robert Simson, of Laura Toorah ; £150 from the Shipwrecked Mariners' Society ; £346 6s 8d, proceeds of bazaar held at Colinsburgh, under the auspices of Lady Lindsay and others; and £400, proceeds of a sale of works of art in Edinburgh. These funds have been invested by the trustees, partly in Government stock and partly on heritable security. Allowances were voted to the bereaved according to their several circumstances, but, generally speaking, at the rate of 4s per week to each widow, 1s 6d to each child under fifteen years of age, and 3s to other dependants. In addition to these allowances, sums varying from £40 to £140 were paid to the relatives of the boat owners, and from £10 to £20 to those who lost nets, and school fees and school books are provided for the children attending school. At the present time (June 1878) the aliment paid amounts to £10 9s 6d weekly. The trustees for the fund are—Sir Robert Anstruther, chairman ; Provost Anderson, deputy chairman ; Earl Lindesay, Rev. Dr Christie, Provost Watson, and Bailie Sharp, Cellardyke ; Provost Tosh, Pittenweem ; Chief Magistrate Nicol, St Monance ; and Messrs David Hutt and Thomas Murray, St Monance—David Cook, Anstruther, honorary secretary and treasurer. The Provosts of Kilrenny, East Anstruther, and Pittenweem, and Chief Magistrate of St Monance are only trustees *ex officio.* Ex-Provost Martin, Cellardyke (one of the original trustees) dispenses the weekly aliment in that place, and Messrs Murray and Hutt in St Monance.

The gush of sympathy—generous as it was widespread—far exceeded the most sanguine anticipations ; but no tribute was more touching and beautiful than on the part of the inhabitants of Lynn. We saw their Christian feeling at the open grave ; but it did not end here, for almost on the day the resolve was taken to erect some fitting memorial where the eight sleepers had been gathered side by side in the " City of the Dead." A committee was formed, and in all about £45 was raised.

Several designs were submitted to the committee, who decided
upon one of a rather striking character, viz., a *fac simile* in
stone of the fishing boat "Beautiful Star," akin to the monument
over the grave of Grace Darling in Bamborough Churchyard.
The mason work is executed in Kenton stone.   The model of
the boat is 6 feet 2 inches in length from stem to stern, and
weighs about $1\frac{1}{2}$ tons.   It is fixed on chocks, placed upon the
upper platform of a fine pedestal of three steps or tiers, the
whole weighing nearly 7 tons.   The stones immediately under
the boat bear the following inscription :—At the bow—" This
monument was erected by public subscription to the memory
of eight Scotch fishermen drowned on the Norfolk coast in the
November gale, 1875."   Beneath the stern is—" Life, how
short !   Eternity, how long !"   On either side are engraved
the names of the deceased fishermen, and dates of their birth,
in the following order :—On the north side—" David Allen,
born 28th August 1827 ; Alexander Duncan, born 7th June
1829 ; Thomas Lawrie, born 3d October 1854 ; Thomas Fyall,
born 27th June 1851," and beneath, the inscription—" When
the shore is won at last, who will count the billows past ?"   On
the south—" James Paterson, born 18th July 1826, and his
son Robert Paterson, born 31st October 1857 ; David Davidson, born 1st February 1852; William Paterson, born 18th
January 1830," and beneath—" While we linger on the shore
of life a wave wafts us to eternity."   The boat is inscribed
" Beautiful Star, K.Y., 1298, St Monance," and is intended as
a representation of her in her wrecked condition, as she was
towed into Lynn by the screw steamer " Sea Nymph " on
Saturday, 27th November.   The tomb is surrounded by a
neat iron fence.   The cost of the monument was £30.   After
defraying this amount and the necessary additions for fixing
and cemetery fees, amounting in all to about £7 or £8, the

balance of the money raised was sent to the Fifeshire Relief Fund.

On a Thursday afternoon in the following spring, in presence of a considerable number of spectators, the memorial, which is centrally situated among the fishermen's graves, and over that of James Paterson, was uncovered with a brief ceremony. The Rev. P. J. Rollo, Union Baptist minister, having offered up prayer,

The Mayor said he appeared there that afternoon as Chief-Magistrate for the time being, and at the request of the committee who had undertaken the task of erecting a memorial stone over the graves of the Scotch fishermen, whose bodies were interred in the cemetery. The committee had done their work on the present occasion with every imaginable felicity and good feeling. Undoubtedly a great amount of sympathy had been shown and still existed with regard to the unfortunate fishermen whose bodies had been placed in that and the surrounding tombs, and it redounded to the honour and credit of the people of Lynn that much of the sympathy had taken a form in the shape of a sensible provision for the distressed. In the hour of distress, when wives were bereaved of their husbands and of their friends, then was the time when such acts of kindness were felt. He thought that no greater expression of good feeling could be wished for than that which had been made. The subscriptions which had been raised on behalf of the distressed were received with thankfulness ; and they felt that their departed friends had gone to a place of eternal rest. When it became known to those whose friends lay in those graves that this monument had been erected to their memory, they would feel another spark of gratitude spring up in their hearts, and they would say to themselves— " They were strangers who showed us that act of kindness, but they did not seem to forget that we were flesh and blood like themselves." He thought that all who had met there that day might instil into their hearts the well-known fact that " in the midst of life we are in death ;" and then they would have nothing to regret that they had spent a few minutes that afternoon beside the fishermen's graves.

Mr I. Rix thanked the Mayor, on behalf of the committee, for honouring them with his presence that day. He also thanked the Rev. P. J. Rollo for the appropriate and sympathetic prayer which he had offered; and the promoters and subscribers to the monument for their liberality and the interest which they had taken in the work. He congratulated the sculptor, Mr Bone, who, he said, had spared neither time nor pains in the execution of his task ; and with one and all who had assisted he felt there would be left a lasting impression, as a pleasing reflection that they had carried into effect that truthful charitable maxim—" Do unto others as ye would be done unto."

The Rev. P. J. Rollo then delivered another short prayer and a benediction, and the inauguration was completed by the removal of the Union Jack, with which the monument had up to that moment been covered.

On Thursday evening Mr Rix, secretary of the committee, telegraphed to the Rev. D. L. Foggo, of St Monance, Fifeshire, that the monument had that day been unveiled by the Mayor of Lynn, and the following telegram was received in reply :—

" Your kind communication gratefully received. Accept my thanks on behalf of my afflicted parishioners. We are truly thankful for your kindness and sympathy. May God reward with his blessing all the good people of Lynn."

In addition to these calamities, in which the crew or most of the crew perished, the tale of sorrow in Cellardyke is continued in the ever present danger of dipping or tacking the lugger sail. Thus it was on the 30th of July 1856, when the corn fields of Fife were rejoicing in the first tint of harvest, from which his eye had just been turned with kindling interest, that the devoted young fisherman, Alexander Dick, was tossed into the sea and drowned, the occurrence being so sudden that the young friend who shared the herring venture scarce caught a glimpse of his upturned face sinking beneath the waves. He shared the fate of a beloved brother, a presentiment which had haunted him for years. " I know I will be drowned one day," he would say in a trusting moment. " Then how do you go to sea ?" remarked a friend. " I am not afraid ; God numbers our days, and Heaven is as near to us at sea as it ever is or can be on land," was the heroic reply.

Again, but this time while the stormy North Sea was still dark with the morning shadows, on Monday, the 21st of December 1864, a young man of singular promise, David Gellatly, was on duty at the haulyards, when, as if cut by the scissors of fate, the tackle slipped, and he was thrown over the gunwale to disappear once and for ever. He was about four-and-twenty, an only son, and as such the stay and solace of the grey hairs that were left to go down in sorrow to the grave. Nine years later the same gloomy sea witnessed another tragedy, the victim being John Wood, who also fell a martyr to duty. His father and other near and dear friends saw him suffer, and heard his last farewell. He had been but ten days married, when the altar was exchanged for a grave in the raging sea. In the fisher homes there is never a more cherished and sacred possession than the beautiful " In Memoriam " cards, which tell of the " loved and lost." They are usually inscribed with some valedictory verses, composed by some relative or friend, of which the following is an example,

selected for its reference to this calamity, which occurred on
the 10th day of December :—

> 'Twas on a dark December night,
>   Eighteen hundred and seventy-three,
> From Cellardyke—their spirits light—
>   Full fifty crews went out to sea.
>
> A hardy, persevering race,
>   As e'er drew treasure from the sea ;
> From May's bright light their course they trace,
>   And swift as birds on wing they flee.
>
> The "Anna" bounds across the main,
>   As fiery steed sweeps o'er his course ;
> The waters beat her bows in vain,
>   Then yield to her superior force.
>
> With buoyant hopes and prospects bright,
>   Her brave crew, all unused to fear ;
> No tempest lashed the waves that night,
>   Nor dream they there is danger near.
>
> The ground is reached, each at his post,
>   To set their lines they now prepare—
> A father's pride, a mother's boast,
>   A fond wife's joy—John Wood was there.
>
> A splash ! a cry ! a wild alarm !
>   Yet, though they see him on the wave,
> A father's and a mother's arm
>   Are powerless in that hour to save.
>
> In haste they throw whate'er will float,
>   Her course they change, the sail they tack ;
> Alas ! too late to reach the spot,
>   Though eagerly they urge her back.
>
> In agony each nerve they strain—
>   The bravest hearts could do no more ;
> Yet all their efforts are in vain—
>   "Farewell !" he cries, and all is o'er.

The father's heart, frantic with grief,
   Is bowed beneath the awful blow ;
Too deep the sorrow for relief,
   The very tears refuse to flow.

To his fond parents' hearts how dear—
   Their every joy and grief he'd share ;
'Twas his delight their hearts to cheer,
   And kindly lift their load of care.

And who can tell the crushing power
   Of grief which wrings the widow's heart
In this afflictive, trying hour,
   From him she loves, so soon to part ?

Each other's hearts, how well they know,
   In childhood they together ran ;
And with their growth affection grew,
   Nor could they tell when love began.

Aye, many a heart to friendship dear
   Now mourns his life's untimely close ;
To all he was a friend sincere—
   Few of earth's sons had fewer foes.

A disaster, painfully suggestive of the black calendar of 1875, occurred in the following autumn, and is thus referred to in a news letter of the day :—The terrible catastrophe in the English seas less than a year ago naturally inspires the most acute and widespread fears for the present safety of the hundreds of Fife fishermen in the south, and the sad news therefore went thrilling through every heart on Sabbath when it transpired that another mariner of old Cellardyke had found a watery grave. The unfortunate victim, William Watson (Jack), had been induced at the very last moment to fill a vacant berth in the Yarmouth bound boat, the " Victoria Cross," of Cellardyke, and which had already rendezvoused at the great herring station. The closing scene is shrouded in mystery, but Skipper Watson is said to have been last seen alive at the wharf by the river side about two hours after the midnight of Sabbath, the 15th inst., and it is only left to conjecture to realise the last struggle—the foot slipping in the darkness, the headlong plunge down into the pitiless waters, the wild cry and the wilder gasp for life, and then the deep river rolling as before with the solemn secret buried for ever in its bosom. All suspense, however, is put to rest by another week, through the recovery of his body in the river on Saturday. The unfortunate mariner had been missing since the morning of the 16th October, when it is only too probable that while seeking his way in the black shadows by the water side in early morning he stumbled over the wharf, and thus, according to the verdict of the jury at the coroner's inquest, was "accidentally drowned." His funeral took place on Monday, when a large company of mourners, including many of his neighbours as well as the seafaring men of Yarmouth, paid the last tribute of sympathy and respect by following the remains to the beautiful cemetery hard by the magnificent old church of St Nicholas, where, through the long generations, unnumbered voyagers rest in peaceful anchorage after the perils and storms of life.

Another sufferer was one of the same boat, and in his fate the sad and weary saying that "Misfortunes never come singly," was mournfully realised, as Skipper James Anderson, Pittenweem, had been drowned in the offing of the Billowness on Saturday, while the next victim, David Doig (Wood), found a watery grave on the following Tuesday. He was one of the crew of the "Victoria Cross," owned by the brothers John and George Doig. It occurred as they were returning from the search for herring bait near the Isle of May. It was a whistling breeze from the sea, with every now and then a blinding shower of snow. In one of these it was thought necessary to reef the foresail, and this had been done, and the crew were resting together, David Doig having taken his seat on an idle spar, fastened, however, to the boat, when one of those sudden lurches, so peculiar to sharp and lively vessels, sent the doomed mariner, swift as a rocket shot, over the lee gunwale into the sea. Next instant his head was seen floating like a buoy on the speckled waters, as the boat darted past in her headlong course ; and then came the dreadful sequel, the upturned hands, the weary look, with none to help or save, as the black waters rolled and whirled over the lonely grave. About an hour afterwards, in the dead of night, the boat arrived at Anstruther, when an early opportunity was embraced to break the mournful tidings to his widow and his only daughter. David Doig, who was about forty-six years of age, belonged to an old and much respected family in Cellardyke, a family of which we read in the parish records of 200 years ago, and he himself was remarkable for those fine qualities of head and heart which secured the esteem and respect of all. The accident occurred some two miles to the offing of Anstruther pier, and about the same distance from the place where Skipper Anderson perished on the previous Saturday night.

The time was 21st of March 1876, and before the end of the twelvemonth a young relative had shared his fate. The melancholy episode may be told as follows :—The young man, Robert Doig, was one of the seven hands on board the deep sea going boat " Southern Cross," Alexander Fowler, master, which sailed from Anstruther harbour in the course of Monday afternoon, 5th of March 1877. The evening in question was passed in the offing at the herring drift, when, succeeding so far in their errand, the crew hoisted sail, with an ample supply of bait, for the cod fishery in the North Sea. All went well, and the great lines were being worked with fair success in the neighbourhood of the Mar Bank, some twenty miles from the Forfar coast, when the crew found themselves helpless in the sweep of the north-east gale. A part of the fishing tackle was still in the sea, and in the hope to save it the anchor was let go ; but as the battle between wind and sea only grew faster and more furious, the crew resolved, some two hours afterwards, to abandon all and run for home. It was midnight, and all was dark as the grave, save when the white-crested billows flitted past in driving foam, but the crew stood bravely to their post. The tall mast was once more ready for the sail, and three of the crew were busy in hooking on the yard when a tremendous sea rolled over the gunwale, and swept all before it into the watery abyss. In that awful moment every man stood face to face with death ; but as the gallant boat rose to the billows those on board could breathe in safety, though it was far otherwise with the three boatmates who had been thrown with the sail nto the sea. Two of these, Charles Marr and Robert Watson, were so fortunate as to seize hold of the wreck, but poor Robert Doig would seem to have been tossed by the haulyards far beyond, as he was never seen again. Nor was a death cry heard in the crash of the storm to tell when the mariner sank in his watery grave. By the disaster only four men were left in the boat, but in a lucky moment Skipper Fowler succeeded in laying hold of Robert Watson, who was clinging to the boom, and the same kindly office having been performed by Thomas Keay for Charles Marr, who had clutched hold of a rope, both men, though not without the greatest difficulty, were taken on board.

In the meantime the storm raged with unabated fury, and hour after hour passed before the saddened and weary crew could recover the sail and wreckage, which had been washed into the sea; but eventually, by the goodness of Providence, this was accomplished, and the boat was tacked for the Fife shore, which was safely reached in the course of Wednesday forenoon. No time was lost in communicating with Dr Christie, the minister of Kilrenny, who was thus called upon to break to the aged widow, his mother, her mournful bereavement; but in discharging this, the most painful duty of his sacred office, Dr Christie was greatly aided by his devoted partner, whose large and loving sympathies on this as on former occasions were in no common measure with the bereaved and sorrow stricken of Cellardyke. Robert Doig was twenty-seven years of age, and his quiet and affectionate disposition made him the favourite of one and all.

We are here also called to place on the death roll the name of John Montidore, skipper and owner of the herring boat "Jacobini," who was drowned in the offing of Stonehaven on the afternoon of Wednesday, the 10th of July 1878. He was on duty at the helm, while the crew were rigging the jib for the softening breeze, when, in the endeavour to assist a landsman, he lost his balance and fell into the sea. An oar was thrown to his elbow, but there is reason to believe that his forehead had struck the gunwale, and so stunned and unconscious he sank into the weary deep. He was scarcely twenty-six years of age, and left a widow and four infant children to bewail his fate. John Montidore's oldest brother also perished at sea, as one of the sufferers in the Cellardyke boat lost in 1865.

And now it only remains for us, by way of conclusion, to note the proud achievements of the century. Looking back on the Cellardyke of a hundred years ago you find the fisher home usually little other than a narrow smoke-begrimed cot—the walls rough and unplastered as the low roof, across which the rafters are seen exactly as they were left at the last stroke of the carpenter's axe. You stumbled over the earthen floor, perhaps more damp and broken than the footpath on the other side of the threshold, as you step to the "creepie," serving for a chair at the ingle side, or to the sea chest under the little window, filled with mysterious green glass, through which the sunshine, so bright and joyous in the outer world, comes struggling and dimly, as through the folds of a curtain, scarce lifting the shadows that all but hide the curious recess or the close bed, and the big wooden press, not forgetting the corner shelf, with its long array of brown dishes and antique Riga ornaments, brought home by the head of the house in the voyage to retrieve the fortunes of net and line. It is true, the neighbours of Anstruther and Crail were no better lodged ; but if it was so in the past the picture is far otherwise in the present, when the domestic arrangements are such as to indicate on every side the home comforts and social wellbeing of the people. Nor is the growth of the town less remarkable. The long street described by Sir Robert Sibbald, and through which the rebel clansmen marched to their midnight foray, retains few if any vestiges of those romantic days, especially in the antique gables and great outside stairs, which at fifty points compelled the traveller to flee for his life into the first open door at every approaching pack horse or sledge cart. But let us not forget that in living memory only two fishermen dwelt in this street to the westward of the Burgh Cross, as it rose on its massive stair facing the Old Tolbooth, or in a section of the town where more than one hundred seafaring families are accommodated to-day. The breezy croft behind Bishop Kennedy's house is at this hour populous Dove Street, and the fine terrace-like lines of East and West Forth Street has also in very recent years given a new and kindlier crest to the shore; but the most notable improvement of all is thus delineated :—

The mason's mallet and the steam crane are awakening the echoes in the interesting project called into birth by the rapid growth of the population and prosperity of Cellardyke. Perhaps, however, any notice of the buildings, present or future, ought to be prefaced by a description of the sites, which we shall endeavour to do.

The situation is indeed eminently inviting, whether looked at in a sanitary or picturesque point of view, being a fine arable field, unbosomed to the sun, edged on the north and east by the public road, on the south by the gardens of Forth Street, and on the west by the barony lands of Anstruther and the old Bow Butts, where the men of the Silverdykes met to shoot the arrow and march out with their gallant young master, Alexander Stuart, Archbishop of St Andrews, to fight and die with him and his royal father on the fatal field of Flodden. The seedling of the enterprise, which takes the first rank as a district improvement, was, we may explain, the application of the School Board to the Superior of Kilrenny, Admiral Bethune, who not only consented to the school site, but also outlined there and then the dwelling-house extension which has now been so auspiciously inaugurated. Never key, in fact, turned at a more lucky juncture, and Provost Martin and other friends of Cellardyke at once embraced the welcome offer, which in due season came to have tangible shape in the beautiful feuing plan prepared by Mr Sang, civil engineer, Kirkcaldy. " But what of the price ?" asks the reader, and our answer is, that at Pittenweem building sites are to be had at twelve guineas an acre, but at West Anstruther, St Monance, and

even in the late extension of Cellardyke, the price was and is
£20 and upwards, which would appear to be the basis of the
new feus, these being at the rate of some eight-and-twenty
shillings a site, but with a full remission of these feudal
casualties which the Anstruther feuars understood some
twenty years ago so well to their cost.

Referring to the plan, we find the extensive field traversed
by a main thoroughfare thirty feet wide, leading from Ellice
Street on the south to the Kilrenny turnpike on the north,
with streets branching to right and left so as to open up the
ground in all directions. The fisher homesteads will, of course,
be contiguous to the town, and here we find the first house
the nucleus of the interesting extension. It is a corner block
with a frontage of thirty feet, while the other allotments are
at least forty ; but this embryo edifice so far exhibits the
principle on which the new street will be constructed. Each
house is divided into two distinct properties, consisting of a
ground and upper storey, with a lofty attic, specially designed
for the repair and storage of sea gear. The section being
twenty-six feet within the walls, is further divided into an
inner and outer room for the accommodation of the family,
who have the further convenience of a front area, ten feet
wide, fenced by a low wall, or parapet, with cellars in the
rear, and a garden filling up the feu, which, in this way, is
twenty feet in width by an hundred and fifty feet in length.
Here, then, on the once silent field a cheerful and busy street is
seen to have a place, with groups of happy children dancing all
day long in the sweetness and the music of the sunbeam. But
in addition to the fisher homesteads, the feuing plan also pro-
vides, in the northern sections of the fields, for self-contained
villas, of which we would only remark here that they will

be unapproached in the neighbourhood, whether for amenity or charming view of sea and shore.

The Public School is situated in the south-east corner, where, as a bog or marsh, the shot fired at the fishermen by Paul Jones was seen to splash after whizz, whizzing harmlessly over the neighbours' heads, and from which a rusty cannon ball was actually taken while digging about the new buildings. The edifice is in the Tudor style, having class-rooms and lavatories in the centre, and the spacious school-rooms for either sex as projecting wings, which, with the ornate details, lend an air of elegance and unity to the design not elsewhere seen in a similar institution in the East Neuk. The teacher's house, a neat villa-like building, stands between the school and Rodger Street, as the new thoroughfare is called, in recognition of the valuable gifts to his native town of the late Captain Alexander Rodger, ship owner, Glasgow. The architect was Mr Currie, of Elie, and the cost to the School Board is about £2500. The new church, which is the earnest, not of the Mission, but of the parish of Cellardyke, is on the opposite side of the " Powcausie " road, where the ground is also within the boundaries of the feuing scheme. The design is cruciform, and in the pointed style, having the front elevation towards the school, where it presents a massive gable, pierced with a great window of three lights, and flanked with tower and spire, which is likely to figure in the " Coasting Pilot " as one of the most striking sea marks on the shore. The sittings are 650 in the nave and transept, and 150 in the gallery—the cost, including the Sabbath school rooms in the rear, being about £3000. This church is so far a memorial of the ministry of the Rev. John Christie, D.D., who succeeded as the eighteenth Protestant incumbent of the parish in the autumn of 1872, but who resigned on being elected five years

later as Professor of Church History in his *alma mater* of
Aberdeen.

Thus much of the shore we now turn to the sea, where new
paths and new harvests have given a crowning fulness to
basket and store. In the days of Queen Anne the historian
counted ten boats in the little harbour, and living memory
has also seen the fishing squadron reckoned by the fingers;
but a brighter day has dawned on the grey old rocks
of " Skimfie," and we cannot more appropriately close our
narrative than with the statistics kindly supplied by Mr
William Gillis, of the Fishery Board. They refer to 1878,
the present year, and are as follows :—

St Monance, 135 Boats, valued at   -   -   -   -   £8277.
　　　,,　　　Nets,　　,,   -   -   -   - 12,900.
　　　,,　　　Lines,　　,,   -   -   -   -   4200.
Pittenweem, 82 Boats, valued at   -   -   -   - £4926.
　　　,,　　　Nets,　　,,   -   -   -   -   7200.
　　　,,　　　Lines,　　,,   -   -   -   -   2200.
Anstruther and Cellardyke, 200 Boats, valued at   £14,000.
　　　,,　　　　　,,　　　Nets,　　,,   - 19,720.
　　　,,　　　　　,,　　　Lines,　　,,   -   5100.
Crail, 32 Boats, valued at   -   -   -   -   -   £190.

APPENDIX.

Many notable improvements have been wrought in recent years on the Fifeshire fishing boat, and yet, as our narrative but too sadly tells, scarcely a season comes and goes without bringing its own griefs and bereavements to the fisher home. Thus, while our volume was going through the press, no fewer than three gallant men lost their lives in the English seas. Some had conjectured that the calamity of three years before would arrest the enterprise thitherward ; but so far was this from being the case that in the autumn of 1878 Cellardyke sent out as many as fifty-six, Pittenweem eighteen, and St Monance twenty-seven boats to fish the herring at Yarmouth or Lowestoft. The season was again one of storm and disaster, and, turning to the *Fife News*, we read under the date of the 26th of October 1878 :—"Again the wild winds are sighing the sorrows of the sea, and in the old home the big tear is falling over the hopes and joys buried for ever in the deep. In this case the victim is Andrew Lyall, one of the crew of the Cellardyke boat 'Cyprus,' owned by his brother-in-law, Skipper John Watson, which, like others of the Scottish fleet, sailed from Lowestoft for the herring sea in the course of Monday. The weather was and had been threatening ; but cheered by the rising prospects of the fisheries boats had faced the terrors of the night, when the squall once more burst upon them with all the fury of the hurricane. It was in the hour of the wildest conflict with wind and sea that the 'Cyprus,' while standing into the land, was struck by a tremendous wave, which buried the deck in the bosom of the foaming surge. The gallant boat bounded like a strong wrestler from the grasp of her enemy, and each brave man breathed again a thankful prayer for his deliverance ; but there was one hero the less after that terrible ordeal. It was the sad old story : a brave hand is struck in an instant from its last lifehold, and sent to battle, without a chance or possibility of rescue, in the jaws of death, where, perchance, the drowning cry is heard, but scarce heard, ere all is hushed for ever in the silence of the grave. The disaster occurred about four o'clock on Tuesday morning, and in the course of the day the fatal news were telegraphed to Cellardyke, where the deceased, who is about sixty years of age, leaves a widow to bewail his loss. Andrew Lyall was a fine specimen of a Scottish fisherman—strong and resolute as the element, at once his cradle and his grave, but withal as sympathetic and true as the needle which so often guided him through the darkness and the storm."

The next was the Anstruther sailor, John Duff, who was drowned at Yarmouth on Monday, the 28th October. He was one of the crew of the Cellardyke boat "James and Martha," and his fate is painfully suggestive in every circumstance of that of poor William Watson, who perished in the river two years before. His body was recovered on Thursday by an urchin while fishing by the quayside with hook and line. He was a married man, and about forty-two years of age.

The third sufferer was Alexander Watson, skipper and owner of the "Polar Star," of Cellardyke. This boat put to sea from Lowestoft pier on Monday, the 4th of November, and had shared in some degree in the success of the night, when she was overtaken by the dreadful tempest, which burst with scarcely any warning from the northward. The sky was black with the night and the storm ; but the gallant craft sped bravely on till the fairway through the great sandbanks, known as "St Nicholas' Gap," had been all but crossed, when in a fatal moment the boat was struck with a heavy sea, which swept the skipper from the helm, and consigned him without a struggle to a watery grave. This occurred about three o'clock on Tuesday morning, and within six hours the streets of Cellardyke everywhere echoed with the mournful tidings—neighbours hastening to and fro, or groups of wives and mothers weeping for the dead, or trembling, perchance, with the terrors which they could not, dared not, breathe except in prayer. On Lowestoft pier the sorrow, if less obvious to the eye, was not less deep and sincere, as few men have held and deserved so high a place in the esteem and respect of their neighbours as the heroic skipper, who had that day perished at the post of duty and danger. Alexander Watson was within two days of his forty-third year, and his loss has been the breaking up of another happy and interesting household—a widow and five sons in tender childhood being cast upon the guardianship of God.

THE END.